I0812144

DISCOVERING YOUR COMMUNICATION TYPE

DISCOVERING YOUR COMMUNICATION TYPE

THE 5 PATHS TO DEEPER CONNECTIONS AND STRONGER RELATIONSHIPS

JASON VANRULER

ZONDERVAN BOOKS

ZONDERVAN BOOKS

Discovering Your Communication Type

Published by Zondervan, 3950 Sparks Drive SE, Suite 101, Grand Rapids, MI 49546, USA.
Zondervan is a registered trademark of The Zondervan Corporation, L.L.C., a wholly owned subsidiary of HarperCollins Christian Publishing, Inc.

Requests for information should be addressed to customercare@harpercollins.com.

Zondervan titles may be purchased in bulk for educational, business, fundraising, or sales promotional use. For information, please email SpecialMarkets@Zondervan.com.

ISBN 978-0-310-37045-1 (audio)

Library of Congress Cataloging-in-Publication Data

Names: VanRuler, Jason, 1980- author
Title: Discovering your communication type : the 5 paths to deeper connections and stronger relationships / Jason VanRuler.
Description: Grand Rapids, MI : Zondervan Books, [2026]
Identifiers: LCCN 2025054206 (print) | LCCN 2025054207 (ebook) | ISBN 9780310370420 trade paperback | ISBN 9780310370444 ebook
Subjects: LCSH: Interpersonal relations--Religious aspects--Christianity
Classification: LCC BV4509.5 .V36 2026 (print) | LCC BV4509.5 (ebook)
LC record available at https://lccn.loc.gov/2025054206
LC ebook record available at https://lccn.loc.gov/2025054207

The author is represented by Tom Dean, Literary Agent with A Drop of Ink LLC, www.adropofink.pub.

HarperCollins Publishers, Macken House, 39/40 Mayor Street Upper, Dublin 1, D01 C9W8, Ireland (https://www.harpercollins.com)

Cover design: James W. Hall IV
Cover illustration: Jorg Greuel / Getty Images
Interior design: Lori Lynch

Printed in the United States of America

26 27 28 29 30 LBC 6 5 4 3 2

The sun looks down on nothing half so good as a household laughing together over a meal.

—C. S. Lewis

Every night, I get to sit at a table with the people I love most. We talk, laugh, listen, and challenge one another. Sometimes we cry.

It's not *exactly* a Norman Rockwell painting, but it's as close as it gets on this side of heaven.

I dedicate this book to the people at my table: Jodi, Oliver, Isla, and Finn.

Together, we do big things.

CONTENTS

The vignettes in this book are composites drawn from a blend of personal and professional experiences, clinical observations, and common patterns and themes. They are not based upon any one individual, and details have been changed to protect privacy. Any resemblance to actual persons, clients, or stories is purely coincidental.

Introduction

If you want to go fast, go alone. If
you want to go far, go together.
—AFRICAN PROVERB

We just can't communicate."

I have heard this sentiment many times from couples, colleagues, church members, and clients. If I'm honest, I've even said it myself. As a husband, father, and therapist, I've witnessed conversations full of potential for connection fall apart mid-sentence. Not because someone gave up or wanted to fail, but because of a lack of clear communication.

Often, people seem to be speaking two different languages, and neither is fluent in the other. Although they can discuss basics, their conversations become strained when they delve into deeper topics or become serious. Language breaks down, leaving only disconnection and frustration.

Human connection is fragile.

We often talk past and miss each other in our marriages, workplaces, and family relationships. Much like mountain climbers isolated on separate paths, we feel lonely and confused by how we keep missing each other, but we all want to reach the summit that is connection.

We long for that summit in our relationships—to be seen, heard, and understood—but each of us takes a different path to get there. Often, we fail to realize that disconnection isn't always personal; it's patterned.

We lose each other along the way, not because we don't care, but because we don't see how differently we're wired and why we take different paths.

It's like the old mountaineering phrase: "Many paths, one summit."

For years, I've asked clients to describe their communication struggles. The answers usually circle back to the same vague frustration:

> "I don't know. We just can't talk."

That confusion is the problem. Communication isn't just what we say; it's also how we deliver, receive, and interpret what is said. It's layered with tone, timing, emotion, and context. It's rarely straightforward and instead enigmatic. For some, this makes communication seem abstract or ambiguous.

But here's what's true:

> Communication is connection.

And for most of us, connection is everything.

The good news? There is a way forward to greater connection, and it begins with this book.

When you understand your communication type, you gain awareness. When you understand someone else's, you build an alliance.

That's why I created the PATHS framework for communication. It's a simple but powerful model to help you navigate communication with greater clarity, confidence, and connection.

This book will help you:

- Discover your communication type and decode others'.
- Navigate conflict with clarity.
- Communicate your wants and needs without shutting down or blowing up.
- Lead hard conversations with confidence.
- Understand the *why* behind your words and how to grow.
- Spot the difference between healthy and harmful communication patterns.

You may have struggled with communication up to this point. But that doesn't have to be the end of your story.

Let's begin our journey up the mountain, toward one another and into connection.

How to Use This Book

My hope is that this book won't just be a series of chapters you read, but instead a journey that you experience. It's a guide to better understanding yourself, your communication type, and the ways in which you connect with (and disconnect from) the people who matter most to you. Whether you're here because you feel stuck in a broken relationship pattern, feel misunderstood, or simply want to have happier and healthier relationships within your personal and professional life, you are in the right place. Whatever your reason for picking up this book, below are some suggestions to help you make the most of the journey.

1. **Begin with curiosity, not criticism.**

   You will likely recognize both yourself and others as you read this book. That's a good thing. But this book is less about labeling and more about liberating. There's no need to "fix" your type, or anyone else's, because a person's type isn't connected to their worth. Instead, use the opportunity to discover what's beneath your patterns, what drives your instincts, and how you can grow toward more secure and meaningful connection.

2. **Find your primary communication PATHS type.**

   The PATHS framework is made up of five distinct communication types: Peacemaker, Advocate, Thinker, Harbor, and Spark. Each type has both strengths and struggles. There is not a best type. Find your primary type and then read the corresponding chapter to learn how to focus on your strengths and improve in the areas where you struggle. You'll find relatable stories, psychological insights, biblical truths, and practical strategies for greater connection.

3. **Read with others in mind.**

   Reading this book to understand your own communication type is powerful, but reading to understand others' is transformational. As you read about the other PATHS types, think about the people in your life. You'll begin to see them with greater compassion and clarity, which in turn makes space for healing, vulnerability, and connection.

4. **Use the tools, reflections, and scripts.**

   Each PATHS type chapter includes reflection questions and callouts with sample language to help you move from insight to action. Don't skip them. Instead, use them in real conversations at work and home, while journaling, and even in therapy. Growth happens when you move from awareness to action.

5. **Go at your own pace but don't stop.**

This book is designed for reflection and growth rather than speed. Read slowly and reread often. Highlight what resonates and talk through what you are learning with a trusted friend, partner, or coach. Change takes time, but the journey toward secure and wholehearted connection is always worth it.

PART 1

Love does not consist in gazing at
each other, but in looking outward
together in the same direction.

—THE LITTLE PRINCE

CHAPTER 1

PATHS Overview

Mont Blanc and the Five Paths

Mont Blanc is the highest mountain in western Europe. Towering over the rest of the Alps, it's not only stunning but also symbolic—a destination that draws climbers from around the world. And here's the fascinating part: There isn't just one way to get to the top. In fact, there are five major routes to the summit. Each one starts in a different region. Each one has its own terrain, pace, risks, and rewards. Traveling these paths, people eventually reach the same place—just not in the same way.

That's a lot like communication.

Imagine now that five climbing guides and their groups set out to climb Mont Blanc, all on different paths. Each guide comes with different strengths, preferences, and assumptions about the "right way" to reach the top based on their path. But they all have the same goal: for their groups to reach the summit and enjoy the view together.

The first guide is a Peacemaker.

She chooses a scenic, gradual route from the Italian side. It's quieter than the other options. Less aggressive. She avoids the conflict-heavy sections and instead pauses often, letting others catch up, waiting for storms to pass. Her strength is her steadiness. She's not here to race; she's here to journey well.

The second is an Advocate.

He takes the Goûter route, the most popular and direct. He's determined. Passionate. He's the one saying "We've got this" while he laces his boots. He speaks in absolutes, not because he's arrogant but because conviction is how he makes sense of the world. Obstacles are challenges to be pushed through, not talked around.

Then there's the Thinker.

She selects the old-school, analytical path: the Grand Mulets route. It's a little out of the way, but she likes that. She prefers methodical over messy. Every step is calculated. She's the one checking the weather every five minutes, reading maps like Scripture. Her gift is clarity, but emotion doesn't always register on her radar.

Next is the Harbor.

He's the heart of his group. He chooses the Miage route because it's safer for groups. He's always looking behind him, making sure everyone's okay. He carries extra snacks, backup gear, and an encouraging word for anyone falling behind. His strength is presence. He reads the emotional temperature of a team better than anyone else. But he's slower to act if his group feels unsettled.

Finally, there's the Spark.

She picks the boldest route of them all, the Trois Monts. It's stunning, dramatic, and filled with sharp ascents and adrenaline-fueled challenges. She's the kind of person who makes you feel like anything is possible. She's fast, inspiring; she brings the energy. But she can get ahead of herself—and sometimes, ahead of her group.

Now, imagine our climbers are halfway up the mountain, and a storm rolls in. Visibility drops. Wind howls. Tension rises. And each guide defaults to their instinct:

- The **Peacemaker** says, "Let's wait it out. It's not worth the risk."
- The **Advocate** says, "We must keep going. We didn't come this far to stop now."
- The **Thinker** starts cross-referencing forecasts and altitude reports.
- The **Harbor** checks on everyone's emotional state and suggests they hunker down.
- And the **Spark**? They are already scouting for a shortcut up the ridge.

You can guess what happens next: gridlock. They're stuck. Not because they're wrong. Not because they don't care. But because they're all trying to reach the same place a different way and need a different perspective.

But then something shifts. They radio teams on different paths and start to listen to each other's approaches. The Advocate pauses long enough to hear the Thinker's logic. The Spark hears the Harbor tending to his group and slows her pace. The

Peacemaker offers to be the middle ground between waiting and pressing on.

Together, they come up with a plan that honors each of their strengths.

The Thinker sets routes based on data. The Spark helps energize the groups to keep moving. The Peacemaker keeps everyone grounded. The Harbor watches the groups' emotional capacity. And the Advocate becomes the voice that reminds them all why they started the climb in the first place.

Together, the groups reach the summit, not because one guide led the way alone, but because each of them adjusted. Each of them honored the others' paths. And that changed everything.

Here's the point of the story: Mont Blanc didn't change. The destination stayed the same. But the journey, and the experience of it, depended on how well the guides understood their own paths as well as each other's.

In any challenging conversation between you and another person, you might be talking about the same issue. You might want the same outcome. But if you don't understand the path you're on, and the path the other person is on, you'll get stuck in the storm. Or worse, you'll assume the other person is wrong just because their approach is different from yours.

That's how communication works. We all want to end up together, connected at the summit, but sometimes we lose each other along the way.

What if we didn't have to lose each other? What if we could reach our destination together? I believe this is possible.

To reach the summit, we must understand our own and each other's paths.

That's why I developed the PATHS framework: five distinct

communication paths that help you better understand your communication style and the styles of those around you. Together, the five types—Peacemaker, Advocate, Thinker, Harbor, and Spark—form an acronym you won't forget: P-A-T-H-S.

The PATHS Model

The PATHS model exists to help you recognize what route you tend to take, and how others may be climbing beside you (or across from you) with very different instincts. Once you see these differences, you can name them. You can navigate them. You can choose to stop demanding your way, and instead, walk with others along their route for a while.

That's what real connection looks like. Not one person getting their way, but both people choosing to journey forward together.

One of the most powerful ways to improve your communication, not just with others but also with yourself, is to understand your communication path. Think of your communication path as the route you most naturally take to reach a connection. Every one of us is built for connection, but we don't all take the same way to get there. Some of us move toward connection through quiet thought. Others through passion and energy. Some by problem-solving. Others through emotional attunement or relational harmony.

We're all capable of walking different paths, but each of us tends to have a primary route, a preferred way of getting from conversation to connection. To make sense of this, think about accents. The United States may be a predominantly English-speaking country, but not every English speaker sounds the same. In fact, we often form opinions and assumptions based solely on a person's accent. Some accents are distinct. Others are more subtle. But all reflect something about where the speaker comes from.

Being from the Midwest, I'm no stranger to this. Wherever I go, if I mention I'm from South Dakota, I'll inevitably get hit with a "Minnesota accent" impression. And every South Dakotan (all two hundred of us) knows that we don't sound like that. But to the rest of the world, it all blends together. It's a lighthearted example, but it makes the point: When you know where you're from and how you speak, you tend to appreciate it more. It feels familiar. It's your natural rhythm.

Communication paths are the same.

The five paths aren't just labels; they're ways of navigating relationships. They help us make sense of why conversations succeed or fail, why relationships thrive or stall, and how we can adapt our approach to communicate more meaningfully. Each path has its strengths. Each has its challenges. Each represents a valid and valuable way to communicate.

But here's the key: Connection happens when we learn to understand our path *and* someone else's.

Here's the problem: A lot of us don't even realize we're on a unique path.

That's where conflict often starts. We don't understand our own style, so we miss the impact it has on others. And if we don't understand the path someone else is on, we're bound to misinterpret their words, tone, or intent. Miscommunication isn't just about saying the wrong thing—it's about speaking from one path while assuming the other person is on that same path with you.

If you're in a long-term relationship and feel stuck, it's time to identify your path. If you're on a team at work that's missing the mark, it's time to examine how each person communicates. PATHS gives you a simple, memorable way to navigate those conversations. Because communication is not one-size-fits-all. It never has been.

You already know this. Think of your closest relationships. You've likely noticed that the people in your life communicate in very different ways. Some prefer long, thoughtful conversations. Others want quick solutions. Some are driven by emotion. Others by logic. People's tone, pace, vocabulary, and even posture all come from somewhere. Geography, education, family dynamics, trauma history, spiritual formation, personality, and birth order all influence a person's communication.

Much of how we speak comes from what we've learned. And what we've learned gets filtered through our personality as well as our desires and fears. All of this shapes our communication path.

Once you understand your path, you can start to invite others into it more effectively. And you'll be better at joining others on their paths too. In my experience working with thousands of clients, the biggest communication roadblocks come down to two things: not knowing your own path and not recognizing someone else's.

Take Stan, for example, who came to me with two seemingly different problems: "It's my wife and my boss. I can't seem to get ahead with either one of them, and I feel like they both hate me."

Stan went on to tell me that each time he spoke to his wife he found himself floundering because she spoke much less frequently than him. "I have no idea what she is thinking," Stan confessed. "I end up just doing a lot of talking until eventually she tells me something I said doesn't make sense, and then I scramble to make things right."

He continued, "At work, my boss is a different story. He's fantastic and a charismatic leader but rarely digs into anything of substance, and the minute I try and talk about a problem or issue he shuts down."

Stan sighed. "Jason, I want everyone to be happy and like me, but I can't seem to make any progress. I'm kind and try really hard, but nothing is working. I think I'm in real trouble. What can I do?"

Sometimes people say all the right things, but their words still don't land. Why? Because the words don't match their path. They don't feel authentic—like a dad trying to use his teenager's slang and instantly revealing that he has no idea what *rizz* means. I can try to speak in my kids' language, but it's clearly not mine. It's not my path.

However, that doesn't mean I can't walk their path for a bit. In fact, one of the most important skills you'll learn through this book is how to travel along another person's path, temporarily and intentionally, to connect with them in ways they'll receive. Demanding that everyone meet you on your path? That leads to disconnection. But meeting someone where they are while honoring where you come from? That creates trust.

And when you find someone with a similar path, it feels like magic. Like you're speaking the same language. You don't need as much translation. You don't have to explain every nuance. You just *get* each other. That's rare, and it's beautiful. More often, you'll encounter people whose paths are wildly different from yours. If you can't recognize their route or adapt your approach, you'll end up frustrated or misunderstood.

The PATHS model gives you a framework for interpreting what people say and how they mean it, based on their unique path. It's not just about avoiding land mines; it's about knowing how to walk with someone without stepping on their core fear.

Everyone's communication is shaped by their "why." That's where attachment theory comes in. If you have an anxious attachment style, for example, then deep down, you might believe that relationships aren't stable. You fear being left. So you enter every conversation as if it could make or break everything. One disagreement feels like a breakup. One conflict feels like abandonment.

Your communication isn't just about the topic at hand—it's about preserving connection. That's your why. If someone can reassure you that the relationship is okay *before* you dive into the hard stuff, you show up more open. That's the power of understanding your path. You learn how to communicate from security, not fear.

And it's not just about fear. It's also about strength. Your path doesn't only tell you what to avoid; it shows you what you bring to the table. The Peacemaker brings calm. The Advocate brings truth. The Thinker brings clarity. The Harbor brings emotional depth. The Spark brings creativity and momentum.

Here are some examples of well-known people who followed each of these communication paths:

Peacemaker—Fred Rogers

The Power of Presence and Peace

Fred Rogers modeled gentleness, empathy, and calm in a noisy world. In 1969, he addressed the US Senate not with arguments but with heartfelt conviction that moved them to action. His steady presence created a sense of emotional safety and belonging, which is the essence of a Peacemaker.

Advocate—Harriet Tubman

Conviction in Motion

Harriet Tubman risked her life to lead others to freedom on the Underground Railroad. Guided by deep faith and unwavering resolve, she embodied the Advocate: someone willing to speak truth through bold action, even when words failed and the cost was high.

Thinker—Abraham Lincoln

Clarity in the Face of Chaos

Lincoln's Gettysburg Address is remembered for its brevity and depth. Lincoln approached complex issues with quiet reflection, logic, and moral clarity, always weighing the human cost. The Thinker values insight over impulse, and Lincoln is a timeless model of this path.

Harbor—Maya Angelou

A Steady Voice in Stormy Times

Maya Angelou's words offer refuge. Her writing is poetic, grounded, and emotionally resonant; it has helped many find meaning in their pain. She listened more than she spoke, yet when she did speak, she offered wisdom and healing. Angelou is a true Harbor: calm, compassionate, and strong.

Spark—C. S. Lewis

Imagination That Illuminated Truth

C. S. Lewis communicated complex truths with creativity, beauty, and heart. Whether through *The Chronicles of Narnia* or *Mere Christianity,* he sparked wonder and reflection in readers across generations. His blend of intellect and imagination exemplifies the Spark: expressive, inspiring, and joyfully transformative.

All PATHS Lead to the Summit

It's important to remember that no one path is better than another. And your path isn't a life sentence. It's a preference. You might shift paths depending on your setting. A Peacemaker at home might become more of a Thinker at work. A Spark in public might turn into a Harbor in close relationships. Our environment influences which part of us takes the lead.

What matters is that you learn to name your primary pattern and understand your tendencies. Because when you know your path and you honor someone else's, *real connection becomes possible.* That's what communication is supposed to be. That's why we talk in the first place: not just to express but to connect.

If we want to connect meaningfully, especially in moments of tension or vulnerability, we must bring more than just our words; we must bring awareness. Awareness of how we're wired. Awareness of how someone else may be wired. And openness to stretch into unfamiliar emotional territory to make space for someone else's way of relating.

Think of it this way: Your path is familiar ground. It's the route you could walk with your eyes closed. But connection often lives in the places that aren't yet familiar. Connecting with someone in a new way is like walking a trail for the first time—you're a little more alert, a little more cautious, and a lot more attentive. That attentiveness and intention is what makes the journey meaningful.

In the same way, you might remember your first time driving in a new city far more vividly than your hundredth trip to the grocery store. Novelty wakes us up. In relationships, learning to walk a new path on someone else's terms, whether it's your spouse, your child, your coworker, or your friend, is like driving through a new city. You're alert. You're humble. You're aware of your surroundings. And because of that, you're more thoughtful.

Often, people get stuck not because they're unwilling to connect, but because they keep trying to connect using their own language, their own map, their own pace. But relationships aren't about efficiency. They're about resonance. What good is it if I say the perfect sentence in my language if the person across from me doesn't understand the meaning?

That's why the PATHS model is more than a communication tool; it's a relational mindset. It's a reminder that connection requires context. It asks us to consider not only the message but the heart delivering it and the heart receiving it. Because hearts don't all speak the same language; they each speak the language of their path.

When you take the time to understand this, you don't just communicate, you connect. You don't just express, you invite. And this changes everything.

So let this be the beginning of a new way of relating. A way that starts with curiosity. A way that honors difference. A way that says, "I'm willing to meet you where you are, because I value who you are." That's the invitation of PATHS. Not to walk the same way, but to walk together toward real connection.

Lace up your hiking boots and get ready for an adventure. It's time to discover your primary communication type and get connected.

DISCOVER YOUR TYPE

PATHS Assessment

Instructions: For each item, choose the option that best reflects your natural tendency. Be honest and know that there are no right or wrong answers.

The options for each item are:

0: Not at all like me
1: A little like me
2: Mostly like me
3: Very much like me

Keep track of your total points for each section using the numbers associated with each answer.

P (PEACEMAKER)

1. When there's conflict, I naturally help calm things down.
2. I make sure to hear everyone out before I respond or decide.
3. I frequently avoid confrontation, even if it means giving up what I want.
4. I'd rather keep the peace than win an argument.
5. I prefer to share my thoughts indirectly instead of directly.

A (ADVOCATE)

6. When I see something unfair, I feel the need to speak up.
7. I tend to see things as either right or wrong.
8. I'm willing to have hard conversations to stand up for what's right.

9. I often encourage people who are overlooked or unnoticed.
10. I'm both clear and caring when I speak up.

T (THINKER)

11. When it comes to decisions, I rely on logic and clear reasoning over emotions.
12. In conflict, I notice flaws and prefer factual arguments over emotional ones.
13. I can set aside my own feelings to focus on facts.
14. I'm good at explaining complex ideas step-by-step.
15. Others sometimes see me as quiet or guarded until I'm ready to respond.

H (HARBOR)

16. I want people to feel emotionally safe sharing with me.
17. I pick up on unspoken feelings or tension.
18. People often say I'm comforting and supportive.
19. I'm patient in conversations and give people time to share at their own pace.
20. I feel more comfortable listening to others than talking about myself.

S (SPARK)

21. I am known for bringing energy and fun to conversations.
22. I frequently use humor and stories to keep people interested.
23. I'm naturally open about sharing my feelings.
24. I enjoy motivating and encouraging others.
25. I often change topics and lose track of the main point in a conversation.

Now add up your total points for each section and note the following:

- Which section has the highest score?
- Does that seem most like your primary communication style?
- Which section has the lowest score?
- Are there any sections where your total is larger or smaller than you'd expect?
- Think of a person you spend a lot of time with. What do you think their type is, and how does that affect your relationship?

Note that the goal of this exercise is not to tell you what type you are so that you only have to master that type. Instead, it is to help you learn how you naturally communicate as well as identifying areas for growth and connection.

As we continue, we will focus on developing insight into your own type, as well as increased fluency in other types, so that you can communicate for real connection with anyone.

A NOTE ON PSYCHOLOGICAL FOUNDATIONS OF THE PATHS MODEL

There is nothing new under the sun.

—ECCLESIASTES 1:9

Most of what we know about people—why we love, listen, argue, or withdraw—has been said before in one form or another. I have simply gathered what is true and time-tested and given it language that speaks to where we are today. This book stands on the shoulders of psychology, theology, and lived experience.

The PATHS model takes several perspectives into consideration, weaving together psychological research, spiritual formation, and real human stories. While there are many theories that describe how people grow and relate, the following three stand out as particularly important to our conversation. They remind us that we are both psychological and spiritual beings who are wired by biology, shaped by our experiences, and guided by faith.

Here are three of the models I will be referencing in this book:

Attachment theory helps us understand how we bond, depend, and protect. First developed by John Bowlby and Mary Ainsworth, it describes the emotional templates we form through early relationships and the patterns that shape how we experience closeness, safety, and trust. Some of us move toward connection with ease while others pull away, and still others ping-pong between the two. These patterns do not define us, but they often predict how we communicate and how we seek comfort, manage conflict, and rebuild connection after rupture.

The **Big Five Personality Model** is one of the most widely respected and empirically supported frameworks in modern psychology.

It identifies five enduring traits: openness, conscientiousness, extraversion, agreeableness, and emotional stability. These traits shape how we think, feel, and relate. Without labeling or diagnosing, the Big Five describes patterns that influence how we express emotion, make decisions, and engage in relationships. It reminds us that our personality does not dictate our future; it simply illuminates the patterns we can learn to steward wisely.

The **Enneagram** adds emotional and spiritual depth to these insights. It maps nine core motivations, nine ways people seek love, safety, and significance. Each type reveals a different strategy for managing fear and desire, shaped by both temperament and experience. The Enneagram helps us see not just what we do but why, and reminds us that transformation begins when we recognize our automatic patterns and move toward greater awareness, humility, and freedom.

The PATHS framework was born in an in-between space. It is not another personality test or personality typology; it is a way of seeing how our wiring speaks—how attachment, temperament, and motivation become communication. Whereas other models describe who you are, PATHS reveals how you connect. It is deeply psychological but also theological, rooted in the belief that relationships are sacred spaces where truth and grace meet.

My hope is that practitioners and other readers will find the PATHS model both familiar and freeing: familiar, because it honors the wisdom that came before; freeing, because it gives language to what occurs between us, guiding us to the place where growth, grace, and genuine relationship begin.

Beneath it all is this quiet conviction: that every conversation, when offered in love, is a way of returning to the God who made us for connection. It is my belief that revival starts with relationship, and in deep connection we see the true reflection of the person God calls us to be.

CITATIONS

Ainsworth, Mary D. S., Mary C. Blehar, Everett Waters, and Sally Wall. *Patterns of Attachment: A Psychological Study of the Strange Situation*. Hillsdale, NJ: Lawrence Erlbaum, 1978.

Bowlby, John. *Attachment*, 2nd ed. New York: Basic Books, 1983.

Costa, Paul T., Jr., and Robert R. McCrae. *Revised NEO Personality Inventory (NEO-PI-R) and NEO Five-Factor Inventory (NEO-FFI) Professional Manual*. Odessa, FL: Psychological Assessment Resources, 1992.

Goldberg, Lewis R. "An Alternative 'Description of Personality': The Big-Five Factor Structure." *Journal of Personality and Social Psychology* 59, no. 6 (1990): 1216–1229, DOI: 10.1037//0022-3514.59.6.1216.

Riso, Don Richard, and Russ Hudson. *The Wisdom of the Enneagram: The Complete Guide to Psychological and Spiritual Growth for the Nine Personality Types*. New York: Bantam, 1999.

CHAPTER 2

Peacemaker

My friend George is a teacher who is beloved in his school district. People find him gregarious, interesting, and invested in them, which makes it easy for them to talk with him. Although George loves being seen as easy to talk to, he admits that sometimes he finds himself wishing for a break from the role.

Like the time we went on vacation together for a men's trip. George stayed out of most of the planning and instead went along with whatever more bold personalities wanted. This meant that for many things like lodging, food, and even the destination itself, George said repeatedly with a smile, "Whatever you guys think is fine with me."

This seemed to work out fine at first. George is easy to get along with, and so the trip was going well—until the second-to-the-last day when we were deciding what to do for the day. A plan was introduced to do some sightseeing and get back to the hotel later that night. Surprisingly, George spoke up and said that he had hoped to stick around the hotel and have a slow morning and then check out a local coffee shop. But the consensus was to go out, and so the group agreed and George acquiesced.

As we were eating lunch, I sat with George and asked how he was doing, because he didn't seem to be his typical positive self. George told me that he was really upset about the events of the morning and the planning of the day. Frustrated, he said, "I just can't believe they didn't take me seriously when I asked. I've gone along with what everyone else wants this whole trip and just asked for one thing. I don't get it." From George's perspective, his suggestion to stay near the hotel had been less of a request and more of a demand. He struggled to see why it wasn't taken more seriously.

What George didn't understand was that to the group, his request hadn't seemed very serious. He went along with things so easily and frequently that his request came across more as an idea and less as something that he really wanted. I encouraged George to tell the group that it was important to him to check out the coffee shop and see what they said.

When the group knew what George's request meant to him, they were glad to accommodate. George was surprised to learn that he needed to be so bold as to tell the group that something mattered to him, but upon doing so he noticed that the group was happy to oblige.

Do you know someone like George?

The Peacemaker: Seeking Calm in a Loud World

The peacemaker is a harmony-seeking, conflict-avoiding communicator who prioritizes peace and stability in relationships.

Peacemakers value calm environments and often act as emotional stabilizers in their communities.

The Peacemaker is an easygoing person who is well-spoken and simply wants everyone to get along. In groups, this person accommodates others and is happy to put their needs and preferences to the side if it helps the group get along or have an easier time.

How They're Wired

Psychologically, Peacemakers often align with secure or avoidant attachment patterns. They find themselves valuing connection while also fearing the tension that comes with conflict. In Big Five terms, they are likely to score high in agreeableness and emotional stability, which makes them steady and empathetic but sometimes overly accommodating. Their Enneagram echoes Type Nine, which seeks out harmony and belonging yet can lose its voice to keep the peace.

Communication Patterns

- Gentle, agreeable, indirect
- Avoids tension and seeks common ground
- Reluctant to share strong opinions unless safe
- Often listens more than they speak

Core Fear

What if conflict or tension arises and I lose control?

Many times, the Peacemaker's core fear stems from an upbringing or important relationship in which they were told that they were too much, needed too much, or somehow required more work or effort than they ought to. Other times, the Peacemaker had a chaotic and unstable relationship or home environment where they learned that the best way to get by was to accommodate and manage the emotions of the people around them.

Either way, the Peacemaker learned that the worst thing that could happen would be for them to have bigger needs than what someone is able to give, or needs that somehow burden someone else. For this reason, Peacekeepers are careful not to complain or ask for things unless they are in conversation with a trusted ally, and even then, they often feel a sense of guilt or shame for having legitimate needs because their needs have not historically been met by the people they loved.

Strengths

- Creates emotionally safe spaces by remaining calm
- Skilled at de-escalation and defusing tension
- Loyal, patient, and adaptable to others

Challenges

- May placate others for the sake of peace, leading to inner resentment
- Avoids important conversations that feel risky
- Can struggle to assert their own needs or boundaries

Relationship Risk

When Peacemakers avoid conflict at all costs, they often disappear emotionally from a relationship. Their unwillingness to speak up can leave others guessing and eventually feeling alone.

In my experience as a therapist, Peacemakers often find

themselves in relationships and groups where people need emotional regulation from the Peacemaker. While these pairings are initially good matches and can build quick connection, over time, the Peacemaker may find themselves exhausted from accommodating others' emotions and eventually can become checked out, numb, or bitter.

Samantha provides a helpful case study.

Samantha was smart, funny, and easy to get along with. She was early to her first appointment and was genuinely enjoyable to talk with, which prompted me to ask about her relationship during our first session.

Samantha shared that she had been in a relationship with Max for the last two years and that during that time the couple had struggled at times because Max lost several jobs and went through what Samantha called a "tough time."

She said she had done her best to help with chores, bills, and getting him access to resources but that Max still felt Samantha wasn't doing enough to help. When I asked what prompted Max to say this, Samantha looked nervously at the floor and shared that the couple had a fight when Samantha told Max that she was overextended from covering his bills and needed him to help more.

Tears fell from Samantha's eyes as she told me that while she felt terrible that she couldn't do more for Max, she was also starting to resent having to do everything in the relationship. Samantha's friends and family had long felt that Samantha was outworking Max; they couldn't understand why she stayed in the relationship.

Samantha looked at me and said, "Is it bad that I asked for something? I can't keep going like this, but I don't want to fight. I guess I could try harder."

Conversations that require an ask are often difficult because Peacemakers like Samantha will push themselves until they are on the brink of exhaustion before sheepishly asking for help. Unfortunately, because Peacemakers are so accommodating and easy to get along with, it is easy for partners, friends, and colleagues to assume they are okay and cared for, even when they aren't.

Have you experienced a person like this, who was kind and accommodating to a fault? What eventually happened in the relationship?

The Big Idea

Peacemakers pursue calm. But true peace isn't the absence of conflict; it's the presence of truth spoken in love. Without courage, calm becomes passivity.

Peacemakers need a healthy dose of courage to start asking for their needs to be met and their opinions to be heard.

Metaphor

Peacemakers are like water: calm, reflective, and adaptable. But too much stillness can end up being harmful.

Did you know that in as few as seven days, water can become stagnant and, as a result, toxic? In still water, bacteria and algae thrive and eventually turn healthy water into something dangerous.

Peacemakers must remember that the urge to maintain or force stillness can sometimes result in stagnation if they aren't careful.

A Biblical Example

David's men were armed and angry, set on destroying Abigail's household in response to her husband's foolish behavior. Thankfully, Abigail didn't panic and instead gathered bread, figs, and wisdom. With gentle courage, she rode out to meet the men and used words to do what weapons couldn't; this action changed the trajectory of her life. Abigail didn't just keep the peace; she embodied what it means to be a peacemaker in the face of chaos (1 Samuel 25:32–33).

Under Stress

Peacemakers withdraw, become passive, or suppress their true thoughts. They may agree outwardly while disconnecting inwardly. Stress leads to numbing, avoidance, or peacekeeping at the cost of authenticity.

Remember George from the men's trip? George was an example of what happens when Peacemakers get stressed and overwhelmed. Thankfully, George was willing to take a risk and share how he was feeling, but not all Peacemakers take the same approach. Instead, many Peacemakers handle stress by becoming even more passive and accommodating, believing that they must develop a greater capacity to meet others' needs rather than meeting their own.

How to Grow

1. **Practice Assertive Honesty**

   Start small. Say what you feel and need, even when it's uncomfortable. Create a list of needs, including survival needs like sleep, food, and shelter. Build your list from there and notice what needs are not presently being met. Tell someone safe about a need that you feel isn't being met, and make a direct request about that need.

2. **Stay Present in Discomfort**

   Don't disappear. Calm your nervous system without checking out. Tools like breathing exercises, devotions, and meditations can be helpful ways to develop a calmer nervous system.

3. **Trust That Conflict Can Build Connection**

   The goal isn't avoiding conflict; it's navigating it well. Understand that the people who love you well want to help meet your needs, not fight with you about them. Consider the value of conflict in developing connection and self-confidence.

4. **Own Your Inner Voice**

   Your perspective matters. Stop editing yourself to please others. Chances are you have been quiet during times when your opinion would have been helpful. Try sharing a thought, opinion, or experience and see how it's received.

Just Say This If You Get Stuck

"I usually keep things in to avoid conflict, but this matters to me."

WHEN TALKING WITH A PEACEKEEPER

Say This:

- "I value how you bring calm to the room. Can we talk about this in a way that keeps that peace?"
- "I know this conversation might feel tense, but I'm on your team."
- "You don't have to fix it right now; we're just figuring it out together."

Not That:

- "Why don't you ever take a stand?"
- "Stop avoiding the issue."
- "You're too passive; just say what you're thinking."

Reflection Questions

1. When do I disappear instead of speaking up?
2. Why do I fear tension in relationships?
3. What would it look like to say what I need kindly and clearly?
4. How can I remind myself that my voice matters?
5. When has avoiding conflict cost me connection?
6. What boundary have I been afraid to set?

CHAPTER 3

Advocate

When you cut in front of him, you cut in front of me."

A few years ago, my family and I went to London for our first overseas trip. Ever since my kids were young, we have enjoyed watching English Premier League soccer on Saturday mornings, and my kids and I have been Chelsea fans for some time.

You can imagine how excited we were when we learned that we would be able to attend a Chelsea game during our time in London. The morning of the game came, and we made our way to the stadium on the tube along with thousands of other fans. When we eventually arrived, it was immediately both wonderful and overwhelming. There were thousands of people everywhere.

We got our tickets, and as part of the package we bought, each of us received a drink ticket for a soda, water, or beer. We found our seats and enjoyed the thrilling first half of the game. At half-time we filed out of our seats and headed over to the concession area, which was uncomfortably full and a bit hard to navigate. But we persevered and found a spot in a seemingly endless line, standing next to a gentleman who easily stood taller than anyone else in the room.

As we shared stories and told him about our trip, we began getting closer and closer to the front of the line. We were maybe five people from the front when a man walked up and cut in front of me. Being in a foreign country at an event filled to the brim with people, I regarded this as simply annoying and went back to my conversation with our new friend, Tom, but he couldn't let it go.

"Jason, you can't let 'im do that! It's not right. It's your first time at a game and your kids are waitin'. You have to say something," implored Tom.

As a Midwesterner, I felt this test was one I could only pass by smiling and pretending nothing had happened. And so, that's what I did.

But poor Tom could take it no longer. He tapped the man on the shoulder and without hesitation said, "You know you cut. Get to the back of the line."

The man looked up at Tom, seemingly assessing his chances of winning any kind of argument, and quickly moved away.

"See," said Tom. "You have to stand up for what's right. He knew!"

Chelsea lost the game, but I gained a loyal friend that day.

Do you know anyone like Tom in your life?

The Advocate: Fighting for What Matters

The Advocate is a values-driven communicator who leads with conviction and passion. Advocates speak up for what they believe is right, often acting as protectors for the vulnerable and champions for truth.

To be loved by an Advocate is to be protected and defended. I have had the gift of several Advocate friends over my lifetime. They are loyal and principled and are wonderful friends to all, especially Peacemakers.

How They're Wired

The Advocate reflects a blend of anxious attachment patterns and a high desire for justice and clarity. In the Big Five model, they are likely to score high in conscientiousness and assertiveness, which fuels their desire to lead, protect, and repair what feels broken. Enneagram parallels include Type Eight's courage and Type One's integrity, which are both driven by a deep need for things to be right.

Communication Patterns

- Passionate, value-centered, direct
- High sense of justice and moral urgency
- Can be intense, persuasive, or confrontational
- Motivated by protecting others and standing for truth

Core Fear

What if I don't speak up and something unjust happens?

The Advocate's core fear is often experienced by people who have been bullied or hurt—or who have witnessed others being hurt and felt powerless as they watched. Committed to never feeling that way again—and never watching someone else endure that kind of pain—Advocates spend a great deal of time lobbying for the underdog because they remember what it's like to feel that way.

When speaking, Advocates are careful to uphold their principles even if others disagree. They are prone to feel that their actions are justified so long as the action upholds their principles and values.

Advocates can be launched into crisis if confronted with evidence that leads them to believe their beliefs were unjust and they unknowingly became the very enemy they were committed to fighting against.

Strengths

- Courageous and articulate under pressure
- Inspire change through conviction and vision
- Willing to take a stand when others remain silent

Challenges

- Can appear rigid, intense, or self-righteous
- May struggle with listening when passionate
- Risk burnout from constantly carrying their moral load

Relationship Risk

Advocates can steamroll quieter voices or alienate those who disagree. Their urgency to act can sometimes lead them to miss relational moments, making others feel dismissed or attacked.

"She just started talking about how unfair my parents were being." Jeremy was recalling a recent conversation with his partner, Zoe. Jeremy had a difficult childhood and had worked hard to address his past and work through it. He had agonized for months about whether to talk to his parents about it, and when he finally got the courage to speak to them, he found them to be dismissive and distant.

As he sat at a park telling Zoe about the conversation with his parents, she became stuck on how wrong she felt Jeremy's parents had been in their response. Jeremy had hoped to tell Zoe how he was feeling and what he had learned, but the conversation quickly shifted to the injustice Zoe felt Jeremy had experienced and her anger toward his parents.

"What they are doing is so wrong!" Zoe exclaimed, causing people walking nearby to jump. "How could they do that to you, Jeremy?"

Jeremy wasn't sure about that, but he was sure that this was not how he thought the conversation with Zoe would go. He had imagined a conversation that brought the two of them together, but he ended up feeling like he had just told his big sister that someone was picking on him.

Jeremy left that conversation feeling further away from Zoe instead of closer.

Zoe, on the other hand, felt like she was loving Jeremy well by advocating for him against the injustice that had been done.

What felt like fighting to Jeremy felt like love to Zoe.

Can you relate to any part of this story?

The Big Idea

Advocates feel called to speak truth, but truth must be paired with love. Righteous anger without relational empathy creates distance, not change.

Metaphor

Advocates are like torches in the dark: They shine bright, lead the way, and expose what's hidden. But if not tended, they can burn.

In many times and places, torches have been necessary for navigating dark spaces as well as for protection and direction. But torches often involve exposed fire, which could burn someone or create a mess. So it's worth pointing out two things about torches:

1. They are only used in places and at times where they add value. Torches are not helpful in daylight.
2. They need to be carried in a way that protects the carrier and others from getting burned. In a tight space, without protection, a torch can burn the very person carrying it.

Obviously, people are not the same as torches, but the message is the same. For an Advocate to be healthy, they must learn to identify who wants or needs them to advocate and how to turn their advocating impulse off in the meantime. They must also learn to uphold boundaries so the people closest to them don't wind up getting burned.

A Biblical Example

Esther could have stayed silent and had every reason to keep her head down. But when her people were threatened, she acted. She risked her life and approached the king, not as a victim but as the voice of her people. Her words transformed fear into action and injustice into deliverance. When Esther spoke, she spoke for many and her courageous words changed history (Esther 7:3).

Under Stress

Advocates become controlling, argumentative, or emotionally exhausted. When overwhelmed, they may isolate, internalize anger, or double down on ideology instead of staying relationally present.

For anyone dealing with an Advocate under stress, it helps to acknowledge the perceived injustice that the Advocate feels they must fight for and give them permission not to fight. Sometimes the thing Advocates need most is to have a day off.

How to Grow

1. **Lead with Curiosity, Not Just Conviction**

   Listening deepens your message. Advocates are often quick to notice injustice and then act from there. While this is both loyal and protective, it also means that sometimes Advocates attack when they should have listened instead. Growing as an Advocate means sticking around long enough to hear the whole story and then deciding what to do next. Consider the following quote, widely attributed to Viktor Frankl: "Between stimulus and response there is a space. In that space is our power to choose our response. In our response lies our growth and our freedom."

2. **Pair Passion with Patience**

   Urgency isn't always effective. Timing matters. Sometimes, advocating well means waiting for the time and place where the message is most likely to resonate with those who need to hear it.

3. **Create Space for Other Voices**

   Advocacy is stronger when it includes multiple voices. An Advocate who speaks alone is like a person with a bullhorn.

Whether or not your message is accurate, the louder you are, the more likely you are to silence others who might need to use their voices.

4. **Rest from the Weight of Always Being Right**

You are more than your cause. Your worth isn't tied to your output. You are not required to speak out against every injustice.

Just Say This If You Get Stuck

"I care deeply about this, and I want to understand your perspective too."

WHEN TALKING WITH AN ADVOCATE

Say This:

- "I admire how clear you are; can I add a different perspective?"
- "I know that truth and justice matter to you. I want to be honest too, just more gently."
- "Can you say that again softer? I think I understand your point, but I would like to hear it packaged differently."

Not That:

- "You're too intense."
- "Why do you always have to be right?"
- "Why can't you just go along with it?"

Reflection Questions

1. Why do I feel responsible to fix or confront injustice?
2. Where has my intensity created distance instead of connection?
3. How can I balance truth with grace?
4. What is the cost of always being right?
5. When has listening changed my mind or softened my stance?
6. What do I want to be known for: being right, or being relationally wise?

CHAPTER 4

Thinker

"Can we meet today at 4:00 p.m.?"

It's not unusual for me to get appointment requests, but this one was unusually direct. It was followed up by a phone call about thirty minutes later and then another email. Although I couldn't accommodate, I was intrigued.

When I was able to meet with William a couple days later, he showed up twenty minutes early with a notebook, pen, highlighter, and two books he had been reading. I was impressed and said so, but William seemed unfazed.

Instead, he immediately jumped into describing what had been happening that day. I stopped him and asked him to start from the beginning so that I'd have better context to understand the problem. William seemed annoyed by the request, but he paused and then started over by saying, "My company has grown threefold in the last two years."

William went on to tell me that he and some friends from graduate school had cofounded a tech company that was set to change the health and wellness industry. He shared that he had worked tirelessly to grow the company by bootstrapping it, putting in long hours and learning everything he could. I believed him. The way William described his company, approach, and goals for the future sounded nothing short of excellent; it seemed in many ways that he was living out his dream.

A bit confused, I asked, "Is that why we're talking? Is there something wrong at your company?"

William paused for a moment and teared up, placing a finger on his wedding ring. "No," he said. "It's my wife. She's thinking about separating."

William had not yet mentioned anything about his wife or their two children but, when prompted, talked about them with pride and joy. It was obvious that they were the true loves of his life. He shared about the goals and dreams he had for them, including the trips they'd take together. It all sounded fantastic, so again, with a bit of confusion, I asked why his wife was thinking about leaving him.

William paused and said, "I guess she's just not happy. She says that we can't ever talk about anything and that I'm too rigid and unavailable. I just can't understand it. We have a nice home and cars, and we take nice trips."

I asked William, "*But do you have a relationship*?"

"She says we don't," mumbled William, almost under his breath. "She thinks we never talk about anything that matters."

William went on to tell me that this had been a recurring complaint in his marriage, but this time he was working harder than ever. He had come up with a plan to read several books about being more emotionally available and felt like it would really help.

"Have you told your wife that you are reading these books, or talked to her about what you are learning?" I asked hesitantly.

William responded quickly, "Not yet. But I intend to after I finish the books and therapy."

What William was missing is what many Thinkers struggle with: emotional depth and intimacy. Thinkers seemingly say and do all the right things, but their relationships can still remain shallow and lack emotional connection.

Can you relate to William's story, or do you know someone like him?

I work with several Thinkers, including tech founders and leaders who are brilliant at systems thinking. They can build companies, budgets, and workflows with remarkable precision. But in relationships, they often run into trouble. For Thinkers, clarity feels like connection, but clarity without emotional presence doesn't translate into relational intimacy.

The Thinker: Seeking Clarity Through Logic

The Thinker is a logical, proactive communicator who operates with precision and focus. Thinkers are goal-oriented and prefer direct, structured communication, relying on their internal logic to navigate challenges. They do best when there is certainty about what's happening and what is likely to happen next. They are gifted at achieving goals and tend to be great chess players.

How They're Wired

Thinkers are often shaped by avoidant or secure attachment patterns, preferring the safety of intellect when emotions feel uncertain. Big Five language would describe them as high in openness and conscientiousness, thriving on analysis, systems, and understanding. They mirror the curiosity and independence of Enneagram Type Five and are driven by a desire for mastery and competence.

Communication Patterns

- Logical, structured, highly analytical
- Direct, proactive, and often high-frequency
- Can appear insensitive or dismissive when emotions are high
- Oriented toward problem-solving, not emotional validation

Core Fear

Will my ideas be understood and respected?

The Thinker's core fear is often rooted in childhood experiences in which "making sense" or compiling achievements was valued above all else. Many Thinkers can recall key moments in which they felt a parent's love deepen based on what they had achieved. Thinkers have also often experienced times in their life when they felt incompetent, intellectually inadequate, or shamed for a lack of knowledge or understanding, which led them to a deep resolve to be right.

Strengths

- Communicates with clarity, precision, and purpose
- Excels at logical arguments, planning, and strategic execution
- Direct, efficient, and solution-focused

Challenges

- May come across as cold, dismissive, or overly critical
- Struggles when communication lacks a clear, linear structure
- Can have difficulty identifying emotions in themselves and others

Relationship Risk

Thinkers can unintentionally dismiss emotional expression, leaving others feeling unseen or unheard. Their focus on data and outcomes may leave others feeling like projects rather than people. This is often exacerbated in relationships with those who value emotions more than facts or logic.

In these types of relationships, Thinkers can find themselves trapped between a need to discuss feelings and a deep fear that they will be inadequate. This leads many Thinkers to withdraw until cajoled into speaking more deeply, at which time they can appear cold or distant, walled off from the emotions being discussed.

Interestingly, many Thinkers have a deep well of emotions to draw from but have not been taught to value it. Under pressure, they struggle to take the risk needed to be vulnerable and share their emotions.

The Big Idea

Many Thinkers grew up in environments where emotions were discouraged or even feared. In some cases, feelings were labeled as dangerous, unstable, or weak. In response, Thinkers learned to stay on the solid ground of data and plans, which leads them to fix rather than feel. They can become overwhelmed by the presence of emotions in a conversation and are often unsure how to respond.

Metaphor

Thinkers are pilots flying a well-engineered plane efficiently and effectively. But sometimes, the person on board doesn't want to reach the destination faster; they just want to know the pilot cares that they're on the flight.

A Biblical Example

Solomon was presented with two women, one baby, and zero easy answers. He didn't flinch or stress, but instead listened and spoke with surgical precision. His wisdom helped him to become a legend, not just because he was smart but because he listened to understand. Solomon was slow to speak and quick to listen, and by doing so led a nation with lasting insight (1 Kings 3:28).

Under Stress

When push comes to shove, Thinkers double down on digging in. When a relationship starts "taking on water," their instinct is to patch the leak rather than discuss how they feel. They may not realize that emotional support, not problem-solving, is what's needed. Big emotions confuse them. They want to make feelings fit into a plan. And if the plan is followed, they expect happiness as the outcome. If someone's still upset, they may feel betrayed by the process or become dismissive: *This shouldn't be happening. We followed the plan.*

How to Grow

1. **Practice Emotional Language**

   Use a feelings wheel. Learn to name and describe emotions, even minimally. Practice by keeping a daily journal to reflect on each day's events as well as what you are feeling. What do you notice about your feelings throughout each day?

2. **Shift Question Style**

   Replace tactical questions with relational ones. Ask "Tell me about . . ." instead of "What's your favorite color?" Craft your questions to encourage further conversation rather than simply an answer. Practice asking open-ended questions and thinking more like a therapist than a detective.

3. **Be Present, Not Just Productive**

   Being physically present isn't the same thing as being emotionally available. Learn to pause your internal problem-solving and be present in the moment. Ask yourself, "Is the person in front of me asking me to solve a problem?" If not, take some time off from problem-solving and shift into listening.

4. **Redefine Efficiency**

   Recognize that efficiency isn't always the highest relational value. Some people value efficiency greatly, but others don't. Recognize that being *effective* often surpasses being efficient when it comes to communication.

Just Say This If You Get Stuck

"Help me understand what matters most to you here, so I can respond with care."

WHEN TALKING WITH A THINKER

Say This:

- "I really appreciate how much thought and consideration you put into this. Can we also talk about how it feels?"
- "You've probably already thought this through. Can I share something more intuitive?"
- "What are your thoughts on the next logical step?"

Not That:

- "You're overthinking everything."
- "Why can't you just listen to me?"
- "You're too cold."

Reflection Questions

1. Why do I get frustrated when people are "too emotional"? Where did I learn that reaction?
2. What makes me feel responsible to always fix things, and is that role still serving me?
3. How can I tell when I'm being logical versus emotionally distant?
4. What if my partner, friend, or child has a different

thought process than me? What if emotional safety, not execution, is their measure of success?

5. What does it feel like when I lean into my emotional side? Is there a lesson here?
6. What might it look like for me to balance emotions and logic during important conversations?

CHAPTER 5

Harbor

Harmony is the person everyone wants to talk to about their problems. She is an amazing life coach who became a life coach after embracing what friends like to call "The Harmony Effect": Whenever she goes to an event, she is quickly bombarded by the people who most need a listening ear.

Recently I was at a fundraising event with a large group of people who were all seated at the same table. When our table was invited to get up and go through the line for food, I noticed Harmony talking to someone in the line. We all eventually got our food and made our way back to the table, but Harmony set her food down and said that she was going to quickly finish up talking to her friend and then come back.

Minutes passed, and the rest of us finished our meals. As the presentation was about to begin, Harmony came back and sat down to a cold plate of food. She explained that the woman she was speaking to was having a really hard time and needed some help. Harmony said that she was glad to speak to her but disappointed to have missed a meal with her colleagues, and she apologized for letting us down. (We weren't let down.)

As Harmony picked at her cold Brussels sprouts, I wondered how many times she had found herself being wildly helpful to someone else while forgetting about or losing herself in the process.

Can you relate to Harmony, or do you know someone who can?

The Harbor: Holding Space Through Empathy and Presence

The Harbor is an emotionally attuned, steady presence who listens with depth and responds with care. Harbors are grounded in compassion and often act as the emotional anchor in their relationships.

As a therapist, I can tell you that many therapists are Harbors. Some of my very best friends are people that you just know immediately you could tell your life story to and they would not only listen but also care.

How They're Wired

Harbors often reflect anxious attachment patterns, learning from early experiences that closeness is earned through care and availability. In the Big Five language, they tend to be high in agreeableness and neuroticism, giving them great empathy but also sensitivity to rejection or disconnection. Harbors echo the relational warmth and self-sacrifice of Enneagram Type Two, along with their desire to be needed as proof of being loved.

Communication Patterns

- Warm, emotionally present, others-focused
- High empathy, low conflict initiation
- Indirect when protecting someone else's feelings
- Often puts others' needs above their own

Core Fear

What if I'm too much or not enough for the people I love?

The Harbor's core fear often stems from a deep fear of abandonment that they have tried to alleviate by providing so much value to others as to make it unlikely they would ever be abandoned.

While this thinking is not inherently wrong, it sets the Harbor up for relationships that may feel contingent upon the value the Harbor brings to those they care about.

What's more, Harbors have a natural tendency to bring out vulnerability in others because they are acutely aware of their own need to be vulnerable.

We often give the gift we need most to others, and Harbors are no different.

Strengths

- Emotionally safe and deeply present
- Skilled in reading emotional cues and responding gently
- Creates a sense of calm and keeps others safe in the storm

Challenges

- May neglect their own needs to maintain harmony
- Tends to avoid conflict, leading to resentment or burnout

- Can absorb others' emotions, losing touch with their own

Relationship Risk

Because Harbors so often prioritize others, they may feel underappreciated if their efforts go unnoticed or become overwhelmed by emotional caretaking without reciprocity.

The greatest challenge to Harbors in a relationship is their insistence that they don't "need" anything. Although Harbors may in fact need less than some, none of us are without needs.

One of my favorite couples to work with has been Vince and Julia. Vince is gregarious, entertaining, and intriguing. He is an analyst at a financial firm where he has grown significantly in his career. He appreciates nice things and is always talking about what he'd like to do next.

Julia is an analyst at a different firm and is kind, emotionally attuned, and deep. She is a Harbor that many people rely on. If someone is having a difficult time, the chances are good that Julia has gotten a call and is helping out in some way.

What brought this couple to therapy might surprise you.

"It's like she doesn't even need me at all," said Vince at an early session. "I mean, she's gone so much helping everyone else. I get up and she's already on the phone, texting while we are eating, and doing so much good for so many people. Even me. It just feels like sometimes she doesn't even need me. She doesn't ever want anything or make a fuss."

What Vince was highlighting is a frequent problem for Harbors. They can become so used to helping everyone else that they lose sight of who they are and what they need. When this happens, the people closest to Harbors often find themselves frustrated, not because they aren't getting anything but because they don't have an opportunity to give back.

Harbors struggle to realize or acknowledge that it is difficult to have relational intimacy without reciprocation.

Because of that, Harbors often find themselves in relationships with one of the following types of people:

1. Someone who is unaware of or unfazed by the inequality of effort in the relationship. This person might be described as a "taker." Whether because they can't or won't, they fail to make any effort to create a more balanced relationship.
2. A healthy person who needed help initially but has since gotten better. When this happens, the healed person often finds themselves in an awkward position: They are no longer in need of help and are also not needed. This person may feel forced to either find a new problem they need help with or else find someone who does need them.

The Big Idea

Harbors create emotional safety through presence, not performance. They hold space for others to be real. But when they neglect their own limits, they become overwhelmed and exhausted, unsure how to speak up without hurting someone.

Metaphor

Harbors are quiet coves during a storm: safe, steady, and calm. But harbors aren't invincible. If a harbor is subjected to constant strain, struggle, or storms without rest and reset, they will flood. Even coves need boundaries, structure, and maintenance.

A Biblical Example

Ruth was on a road with Naomi that seemingly stretched on forever and yet went nowhere. The air was heavy with loss, and every part of her wanted to turn back like she had been told to—but Ruth pressed on because love called her to continue. She didn't say much, because her presence was her promise. Ruth stayed rooted with quiet strength in support of Naomi, which became the foundation for generations to come (Ruth 1:16).

Under Stress

Harbors withdraw under stress, feeling overwhelmed by others' pain. They may shut down or begin to silently resent the very people they care for. Their desire to protect others can prevent them from expressing their own needs, leading to internal emotional backlog.

You can tell a Harbor is stressed not by what they say, but instead by how they carry themselves. Unfortunately, many Harbors prefer to suffer in silence, so it's tough to spot when they're struggling.

Look for them to show up with less energy, resolve, and creativity when they are having a hard time, and know that oftentimes, what is most helpful to a Harbor when stressed is permission to take a day off from caring for everyone else.

How to Grow

1. Name Your Own Needs

You can't keep pouring from an empty cup. Self-awareness is not selfish. Harbors should regularly ask themselves, "Who am I allowing to pour into me so I can pour into others?"

2. Initiate Honest Conversations

Speaking up isn't a betrayal of love; it's a form of it. People who love you want to hear your voice and what you have to say. Silence isn't golden; it separates.

3. Practice Emotional Boundaries

You can feel with someone without carrying their feelings *for* them. The ones who can help the most people are those who are experts at drawing a line between their feelings and other people's feelings.

4. Receive Care as Much as You Give It

Vulnerability goes both ways. Let others show up for you too. If you are in a committed relationship, this is vitally important. Your partner needs to know how to love you, not just for your sake but also so they have purpose in the relationship. Withholding your needs doesn't make things better; it makes them bitter.

Just Say This If You Get Stuck

> **"I want to be here for you, but I also need space to be honest about how I'm doing."**

WHEN TALKING WITH A HARBOR

Say This:

- "I see how deeply you feel this, and I want to be careful with it."

- "You don't have to rush. Your insight matters; take your time."
- "Tell me what you're thinking. I'm listening."

Not That:

- "Why are you so sensitive?"
- "Can you just get to the point?"
- "This isn't that big of a deal."

Reflection Questions

1. Why is it hard for me to ask for help?
2. What are the emotional costs of always being the strong one?
3. Where do I avoid conflict in the name of peace?
4. How can I share my feelings without fearing it will hurt someone?
5. When has my being present helped someone heal?
6. What do I need from others in order to feel emotionally safe?

CHAPTER 6

Spark

What first drew Pete to his wife, Veronica, was now the very thing that made him feel alone.

Veronica was the kind of person who lit up every room she entered. Pete often joked that people didn't fall in love with Veronica; they got caught in her orbit. Veronica looked at each new person she met as a soon-to-be friend. She was spontaneous, charismatic, and expressive. On good days, Pete and Veronica felt as if they were living out movie scenes full of impromptu trips, laughter, and fun.

But on the days when things got hard, Veronica was different. Instead of being her expressive self, she instead withdrew both physically and emotionally. If Pete brought up something serious, Veronica would change the subject, make a joke, or, if pushed, suggest that "we just have fun and not take everything so seriously."

This was especially hard for Pete, a Harbor, who was built for depth and meaningful conversation. Over time, Pete began to feel that he had to earn Veronica's attention with excitement, and that anything heavier than laughter and fun would drive her away.

But Veronica wasn't trying to avoid Pete; she was avoiding herself. Veronica grew up in a home where conflict was frequent, and whenever it arose, people either exploded or exited the conversation. As a result, Veronica learned that fun and excitement were safer than feeling. Although this instinct now made her magnetic, it also kept her disconnected from the person she loved most.

Everything changed for Veronica and Pete in a couple's session when Pete finally said, "I don't need fireworks or excitement. I just need you." For the first time, Veronica learned that avoiding discomfort was costing her depth and that true connection wasn't about performing but about being present.

The Spark: Lighting Up the Room Without Burning Out

The Spark is a creative, energetic communicator who brings warmth, enthusiasm, and new ideas to every conversation. Sparks thrive on emotional connection and expression, often inspiring others with their spontaneity and authenticity.

A Spark is the person you want to have with you on a trip, in your office, or in your family. They are driven, fun, and entertaining to be around. They are the life of the party and the person who can swing the emotional energy of the room.

I am blessed to have several good friends who are Sparks, and it's been such a gift to have them in my life. Whenever we talk, they are able to pick out the positive and breathe life and new energy into old ideas.

How They're Wired

Sparks often embody secure or avoidant attachment patterns that seek joy, freedom, and possibility even when pain feels unavoidable. In the Big Five language, they are high in openness and extraversion and are energized by creativity and movement. The Enneagram Type Seven reflects their core motivations, which are to reframe pain into hope and to keep life vibrant.

Communication Patterns

- High-energy, emotional, spontaneous
- Uses humor, stories, and metaphors to connect
- Speaks freely and passionately
- May suddenly change topics or interrupt due to excitement

Core Fear

What if my light is too much (or not enough) for the people around me?

Sparks care a lot about how they are received by others because, in their mind, they want to give everyone exactly what they want. Natural performers, Sparks are often grown-up versions of what therapist and author Claudia Black would call "The Hero Child."[1]

Sparks learned early on in life that to thrive in their family, they must placate others rather than discuss problems. From that upbringing, Sparks learn how to perform to win others over and tend to value the experience they bring to others more than having a shared experience.

What keeps the Spark up at night is a fear that they might someday be told that they are either too much or not enough for others. Sparks can feel deeply sidelined by rejection and struggle with internalizing it to the point that it affects how they see themselves.

For many Sparks, it may feel like their worth is only as good as their last performance.

Strengths

- Brings optimism and emotional vibrancy to interactions
- Connects quickly and authentically with others
- Creative problem-solvers who infuse energy into stuck situations

Challenges

- Can dominate conversations or derail focus
- Struggles with follow-through and emotional consistency
- May avoid emotional pain by performing or distracting

Relationship Risk

Sparks may be adored for their charisma, but their emotional unpredictability can confuse others. Their tendency to avoid hard conversations may prevent deeper trust from forming.

A classic problem that I see in relationships with a Spark is this dynamic:

> If you only knew them the way I do, you wouldn't like them as much.

I observed this with a couple from Los Angeles who had been married for some time. Emily and Brad were the couple that everyone wanted to be like. They had a seemingly perfect family with two children, a large house, nice cars (including a Porsche that I'd be happy just to sit in once), and a thriving business.

Brad was a Spark and the life of the party. He could entertain and connect with nearly anyone and was always moving, creating, and ideating. Emily was not. Emily was a Harbor and was deeply attuned to others' needs and wants, including Brad's.

As Brad had built his business, he'd experienced several difficult times, both professionally and personally, and even had an emotional affair. Although these difficult seasons were the result of Brad's actions, Emily found herself in the driver's seat of the cleanup and often had to step in and save the day while Brad went on to the next event.

When I began working with this couple, it was easy to see why everyone liked Brad. He was funny, intelligent, and inspirational. But there was another less polished side to him, and Emily lived with it. While everyone else celebrated Brad for his achievements and energy, only Emily knew what it cost to maintain that image.

Initially, Emily said nothing because she did love Brad and Brad was fun. But over time, Emily began to feel like she was responsible for much of Brad's success—as well as the cleanup of his failures—while only he got any credit.

Together, we worked to find a connection point where Brad could still be his energetic and fun self while improving his follow-through and developing integrity.

The breakthrough for Brad was learning that healthy relationships require and thrive with accountability.

The Big Idea

Sparks light up rooms, but real relationships require staying power. Inspiration is powerful, but intimacy grows when we stay present even when the light dims.

Metaphor

Sparks are campfires: inviting, energizing, warm. But fires need tending or they either burn out or burn too hot.

A Biblical Example

Peter was the first to speak up, the first to jump out of the boat, and the first to declare his loyalty even though he later fell flat. Jesus called Peter "the rock," because even in the midst of Peter's impulsiveness, his heart burned with boldness, and he couldn't help but go first. In the end, it was Peter's voice that sparked the first sermon in the church and set the world on fire with grace and love (Acts 2:14).

Under Stress

Sparks may either overfunction to keep the mood light or else shut down when emotions feel too heavy. They may perform instead of process, using charm to bypass vulnerability. Disconnection can feel like rejection, causing them to seek validation instead of real presence.

How to Grow

1. Be Present, Not Just Positive

Stay through sadness. Depth builds trust. It is important to be able to sit in difficult emotions occasionally. If you don't, people may feel like they only have a shallow relationship with you.

2. **Embrace Silence as Connection**

   You don't need to fill every space. Practice meditating, either in the morning or at night, and get comfortable with silence. Silence is needed for deep reflection and conversations.

3. **Learn to Linger with Emotion**

   Not everything has to be solved or reframed right away.

4. **Show Up with Consistency**

   Let your presence, not just your energy, build safety. Think of your energy less as being *ready* to spring into action but instead as being *willing* to spring into action.

Just Say This If You Get Stuck

"I want to share this joy with you, but I'll stay if it gets hard too."

WHEN TALKING WITH A SPARK

Say This:

- "I love your energy; can we slow down just a little to stay connected?"
- "You bring so much life to this. Can I add a couple of ideas that I've had?"
- "Your ideas are really inspiring. What matters most to you in all this?"

Not That:

- "You're doing way too much."
- "You never stop talking or moving."
- "You need to be more serious."

Reflection Questions

1. What do I do when the room gets heavy?
2. Why do I feel responsible for keeping everyone happy?
3. How can I be emotionally consistent without dimming my light?
4. When have I avoided a hard conversation to keep things fun?
5. What would it look like for me to stay through discomfort?
6. Who helps me feel safe enough to slow down and be real?

CHAPTER 7

Attachment and PATHS

Raise your hand if you've ever shown up to an important conversation feeling timid, unsure, or even scared. If your style is to never rock the boat and always stay neutral—being Switzerland in the conversation. If you soften your voice, shrink your presence, speak in maybes, ask instead of assert, and assume you probably won't get what you want. If you spend more time managing other people's emotions than expressing your own. If you're more of a listener than a speaker, yet still long to be heard.

You're not alone. Many of my clients have felt the same way. I have too.

What you're experiencing is the voice of *anxious attachment* in conversation. And once you understand how attachment styles work, so much of this begins to make sense.

Attachment theory is the idea that our early relationships with our primary caregivers shape the way we connect with others, both emotionally and communicatively, for the rest of our lives. The foundational research came from 1950s studies in which researchers observed how children responded when their parent left a room.[1]

Some kids became visibly distressed. They cried, panicked, and were difficult to soothe. This group didn't trust that their parent would return or be consistently available. That became known as **anxious attachment**—the belief that relationships, even the most important ones, might not last.

Other children seemed indifferent—unbothered by their parent's departure as well as their return. This reaction became known as **avoidant attachment**—a style marked by self-protection, independence, and the belief that closeness leads to pain.

Then there were the kids who enjoyed being with their parent but were also fine when the parent stepped away. They were confident, calm, and trusting. This is **secure attachment**—the sense that people can be counted on and that everything will be okay.

Later, researchers identified a fourth style: **disorganized attachment**, often the result of trauma or neglect. Children with this attachment style displayed a mixture of anxious and avoidant behavior. They longed for connection but were also deeply fearful of it—confused by caregivers who had been sources of both comfort and harm.

Below is the typical breakdown of attachment styles:[2]

- 50 percent of people are securely attached
- 20 percent are anxious
- 20 percent are avoidant
- 10 percent are disorganized

Now, why does this matter for communication? Because your attachment style doesn't just affect your relationships. It affects your *voice*. It's hard to speak up when you fear closeness or the loss of relationship.

This is true at work, school, and home—including in parenting. Your attachment style is the *why* underlying your communication. It's like the old box of childhood photos hidden away in your attic—evidence of how you experienced childhood. It's apparent in the way you introduce yourself to others and talk about what you do.

And although many try to run from it, deny it, or wrestle with it, one thing is true: If you don't acknowledge and address your attachment style, it often ends up creating the scenario that you dread the most.

For instance, without insight and effort, anxious attachment can lead to constantly seeking validation and reassurance, which can ultimately lead a partner to reject you not because you aren't enough, but because you don't know that you are.

It pays to understand your attachment style and to work toward more secure attachment if you aren't already securely attached.

Let's look at some of the ways attachment styles affect communication in relationships.

Anxious Attachment

If you're anxiously attached, you may fear conflict, not because you're incapable but because you're afraid of losing someone. That fear can shape every word you say.

As someone who is anxiously attached, I can tell you that for a large portion of my life, I looked at relationships through the lens of what I was afraid to lose rather than what I could possibly gain. This meant that many times, I would avoid holding others accountable in any way and instead assume all responsibility.

Jaxon had a similar experience. He had been in several relationships that ultimately resulted in messy breakups he regretted. After these relationships ended, Jaxon thought back through each relationship and could now see that there were moments when he should have seen obvious red flags but was instead too caught up in his own fear of rejection to say anything.

Jaxon's primary communication type was Peacemaker, so he not only wanted to communicate in ways that kept everyone happy but also, because of his attachment style, deeply feared conflict that could lead to rejection or abandonment.

When I asked one day about his most recent relationship, Jaxon said that he wished he would have paid attention to the following:

1. His partner did not keep her word and he never brought it up.
2. There was no accountability in the relationship.
3. Jaxon shared needs and wants frequently but they were not met.
4. Jaxon frequently sought validation and reassurance but was not given any.

That day in my office, Jaxon realized that he had been blinded by pain from the past and that it had caused him to miss some obvious problems.

Together we worked to help Jaxon find a more secure way of communicating, which looked like:

1. Being clear about intentions, wants, and needs.
2. Avoiding general, abstract, or unclear language related to his emotions.
3. Explaining his actions less and developing more confidence.
4. Listening and remembering when someone assured him and validated his emotions.

By doing all of this, Jaxon began to move toward more secure attachment and healthier relationships. Over time, he learned that he was worthy of love and that others were worthy of hearing his true feelings.

Instead of approaching conversations thinking, *How do I make it so this person doesn't get mad or doesn't leave me?*, Jaxon learned how to approach conversations from a more confident position of self-love and objectivity.

Avoidant Attachment

If you're avoidantly attached, you might resist emotional vulnerability not because you don't care but because closeness feels dangerous. That defensive posture can make your communication seem cold or rigid.

Avoidantly attached people often get a lot of harsh criticism and feedback. This is due in part to the damage they can do to anxiously attached people as well as to their lack of awareness of the pain they might cause. However, avoidantly attached people are really just anxiously attached people who refuse to take a risk. Instead of seeking relationships to validate their worth, avoidantly attached people protect their self-worth from relationships that might crush it.

Jackie came to see me after a particularly messy exit from her company. Jackie had started the business of her dreams with her best friends, and just as the company was beginning to experience significant growth and momentum, the board voted to remove her from her position.

Jackie was absolutely destroyed by this news and shocked to find that the people she considered some of her best friends felt she was cold and distant. She had always had a difficult time making friends and being vulnerable but thought she had finally succeeded. She explained that it had not been easy. It had taken her a great deal of work and courage to maintain the relationships with her friends when, at times, it felt easier to run away and start over.

Jackie asked me to imagine her surprise when she finally let her friends into her inner world and they rejected her all the same. Sitting in my office, Jackie said, "See, this is why I don't have relationships. All that happens is you get hurt."

In that moment, Jackie was more right than wrong. She had a history of choosing people who were ultimately less available than her, and after hesitating to let them in but finally doing so, Jackie found that many of them were uninterested after waiting so long.

Think of it this way: Avoidant attachment, if unchecked, is a lot like playing a game for an hour but not knowing any of the rules or the goal of the game. Avoidantly attached people tend to operate based on their own assumptions about themselves and others, aiming simply to keep others from hurting them.

This results in heartache when the other person playing the game decides it's no longer fun to play without knowing the rules, or else the avoidantly attached person decides it's a game they can't win.

The difficulties are compounded when the avoidantly attached person—like Jackie—has the primary communication type of Thinker, because they do not naturally lead with emotions in conversation. This leads to challenges with both communicating and letting others in, not because they don't want to connect but because they have been hurt and find safety in logic.

Together, Jackie and I worked to improve her communication and help her be less avoidantly attached by identifying the following behaviors for her to practice:

1. Sharing some of her feelings early in a relationship.
2. Being honest and up-front when she felt an urge to run.
3. Establishing someone she could talk to who could help her be accountable about the changes she wanted to make.
4. Learning to ask for what she wants and needs sooner.
5. Committing not to exit a relationship without explanation.

Disorganized Attachment

If you have a disorganized attachment style, you may find yourself ping-ponging between overconnection and withdrawal, desperate to be known but terrified of being hurt.

When we talk, we often aren't just saying what we really think; we're saying what our attachment style *permits* us to say. Someone with disorganized attachment may feel at times as though they are at the will of their feelings that day.

Take Luke, a friend of mine who experienced significant trauma and abuse as a child.

Despite a difficult childhood, Luke became a successful surgeon who was well respected and liked by many. However, those close to him often felt as if there were two versions of Luke: one that pursued relationship almost to excess, and another that ran from relationships and was aloof. The people closest to Luke would tell you that it was difficult at times to know which Luke you would get on any given day and that sometimes the version could change by the hour, which made them feel uncertain and uneasy.

Until Luke understood that he struggled with disorganized attachment, he had a series of unhealthy relationships littered with problems, poor boundaries, and unclear exits.

When we sat down to talk at a coffee shop one day, Luke shared with me that he was exhausted from all the work it took to maintain his relationships. Most days he wasn't sure how he felt about them, and he tended to feel stuck between wanting connection and fearing it.

While Luke was an amazing Harbor, adept at making space for others, he struggled to speak his own needs, and as this combined with his disorganized attachment, he often found himself feeling depleted.

Together we worked to help Luke find a more secure voice, which involved him learning to:

1. Identify and develop awareness of his tendency to lean in and check out repeatedly.
2. Establish stability and safety that wasn't based on others.
3. Grow emotional and nervous system regulation skills.
4. Release shame before it grew into the catalyst for ending a relationship.

Luke's story is not unique among those with disorganized attachment.

For people with this attachment style, awareness is the first step, and finding a trusted person or professional to help with navigating all the feelings surrounding relationships is paramount to success.

Secure Attachment

Secure attachment is the attachment style that everyone wants but not everyone gets. For those who are securely attached, communication can be simply a conversation, not a survival strategy. With the pressure of survival removed, communication happens much more freely. However, securely attached communicators sometimes struggle with complacency because they feel that regardless of what happens, they will work things out. Sometimes this belief is used to justify staying the same rather than embracing change.

I have a colleague named Alena who is securely attached—and it shows. She grew up in a fantastic, loving family that did a great job nurturing and caring for her. She received seemingly everything she needed and, as a result, is confident, competent, and caring.

However, Alena tends to struggle with relationships, especially with those who are insecurely attached. For Alena, it's difficult to understand how someone could question their worth or be fearful of relationships. Because of this, if she's not intentional, Alena can sometimes communicate in ways that seem judgmental or even aloof to those who are not securely attached.

Through her work and friendships, Alena has learned to make space for and get curious about people whose experiences have been different from hers. This has allowed Alena to better connect with others and to become a calming presence to those who need it.

Together Alena and I worked to help her embrace secure attachment while making space for others by:

1. Developing an understanding of insecure attachment styles.
2. Understanding and implementing boundaries in relationships where it might be tempting to overwork.
3. Asking questions before making assumptions.
4. Facilitating discussions that matter to others even if she doesn't feel anything needs to be discussed.

Attachment Is the Hidden Driver of Communication

Many of the people I work with come into conversations determined to speak honestly, but when a difficult moment arrives, they find themselves agreeing, placating, committing to things they don't want, or backing down. They ask me, "Why did I say that? That's not what I meant."

And I tell them: "It's because you weren't just speaking. You were speaking through the lens of your attachment."

Someone with avoidant attachment might enter those same conversations and double down. No room for compromise. No softening. Just a firm stance, because yielding feels like weakness—and weakness means getting hurt.

Here's where secure attachment is so powerful: It allows you to participate in difficult conversations without making those conversations about your worth. You're not trying to prove yourself. You're just being yourself.

When it comes to our communication, our attachment style isn't just in the background. It's the foundation. It shapes *why* we speak, *how* we speak, and *what* we believe will happen if we truly show up as our most authentic and honest selves.

Think of attachment as lighting along a path. When we're securely attached, the lights are on. We can see our steps. The path feels steady. But when we're insecurely attached, it's like walking that same path in the dark. Every step feels uncertain. We move cautiously, defensively, or not at all.

Once, I was running near a lake early in the morning. It was beautiful, but the sun hadn't come up yet, and the path was nearly invisible. What should've been peaceful felt unsafe. I couldn't see my next step. That's what communication feels like when an insecure attachment style is activated and the "lights" are off.

So how do we turn the lights on?

We regulate. We pause. We notice the story we're telling ourselves and ask, *Is this a past fear, or a present reality?* Sometimes we must wait for the emotional "sun" to rise before we engage.

This is why it's so important to know your attachment style *and* the attachment style of the person you're talking to. You're likely to feel friction with someone whose attachment lens is different from yours, especially in anxious and avoidant pairings. Understanding your attachment styles gives you the tools to help you stop missing each other and start truly connecting.

As you walk your communication path, remember that attachment lights the trail. And each of the PATHS (Peacemaker, Advocate, Thinker, Harbor, Spark) has a *secure* version and an *insecure* one. Secure versions walk in clarity. Insecure versions stumble through fear.

My goal is to help you find your footing and turn on the lights so that the words you speak will come from truth, not fear.

Reflect

1. Which attachment style do you identify with most?
2. What do you wish people in your life understood about how your attachment style impacts you?
3. Do you suspect that your attachment style influences your communication style? If so, how?
4. If you suspect your attachment style is something other than secure, what steps could you take to learn more?

Further Reading

Levine, Amir, and Rachel S. F. Heller. *Attached: The New Science of Adult Attachment and How It Can Help You Find—and Keep—Love.* New York: TarcherPerigee, 2010.

Johnson, Sue. *Hold Me Tight: Seven Conversations for a Lifetime of Love.* New York: Little, Brown, 2008.

CHAPTER 8

The PATHS Effect

I remember the moment clearly. I was with a couple at a retreat I hosted just outside of Nashville. Gorgeous property, great food, peaceful surroundings—and they were arguing. A lot. Which, by the way, is more common than you'd think at a retreat. Because while retreats often take place in a beautiful environment, what we're really there to do is bring to the surface stuff that's been buried. And when a couple has been avoiding important conversations, finally having them can stir up a lot—no matter how scenic the backdrop.

This couple? I absolutely adored them. They loved each other too. But they just could not connect in conversation. You know the feeling—when no matter how much you love the person, the minute you start talking about something that matters, the conversation unravels.

Over time, the questions get deeper: *Why does this keep*

happening? What is it about me—or about the other person—that creates this dynamic? Maybe you've even thought, *Why don't I argue like this with anyone else?* Well, here's the thing—the more meaningful the relationship, the higher the stakes, and the more exposed our wounds and wiring become.

Your attachment style doesn't stay in the background during conflict; it takes center stage. So does the shadow side of your communication path.

What drew you to your partner (the thing you admired in them) can become the thing you dread. I can't count how many times I've heard a client say, "I loved that they were outspoken when we met. I'm passive, I don't speak up, and they were bold and confident." And then, a few years in: "I can't stand how controlling and intense they are."

This is why understanding each other's *communication path* and *attachment style* matters in our relationships. Because if we don't, we end up fighting about not just what's being said but also *how* it's being said. We argue over whose path is right. And if we don't even realize we're on a path, how can we hope to navigate it?

Whether in couples, teams, or friendships, we're often drawn to difference. It's compelling. It's exciting. And difference can be beautiful. But it can also become frustrating. What initially drew us together becomes the thing that pushes us apart.

That's where the work of identifying your path becomes transformative. When you know your path, you start to notice the paths of others. You begin to understand how to meet in the middle, not by compromising who you are but by adapting your approach.

Let's say you're an Advocate who is passionate, bold, and justice-oriented, and you're in conversation with a Thinker who is practical, grounded, and logic-driven. You come in with feeling; they come in with facts. You lead with passion; they measure with precision. It feels like you're speaking two different languages. And in a way, you are.

But if you can understand where they're coming from and what they need from you—not just react to how they're communicating—the conversation shifts. This isn't about losing your voice. It's about learning how to speak *so they can hear it.*

Each path has a zone of genius, to borrow a phrase from psychologist Gay Hendricks's book *The Genius Zone*. And each path also has blind spots. Your job isn't to be perfect in every area. It's to know what you bring to the table and where you need support.

So how do you spot a path in someone else? You listen—not just to what they're saying but to what they're *not* saying. How do they start conversations? What do they avoid? What are they asking for beneath their words?

A good shortcut is to ask yourself two questions:

1. What do they need most from me in this conversation?
2. What do they fear most about having this conversation?

When you can answer those, you're able to start communicating with compassion instead of just reaction.

Let's say someone has an anxious attachment style. They might fear that bringing up a point of conflict could cost them the relationship. If you lead by saying, "Hey, we're good. This is a hard conversation, but you and I, we're solid," it calms the alarm. It turns the lights on.

That's the goal here: not to agree on everything, but to create *light*—clarity, safety, connection.

Being aware of others' paths also helps when assigning roles within a group. An Advocate might thrive in a bold, outward-facing leadership role. A Peacemaker might be better at building relational bridges behind the scenes. Understanding the paths can help a person place others—and themselves—where they'll thrive.

What follows isn't a communication script. It's a relational map. And when you know your map, you stop walking in the dark.

When we start to recognize our patterns and understand others', communication shifts from a struggle to a skill. And the more you practice it, the more fluent you become.

Yes, this takes practice.

But I've watched it change teams. Marriages. Parenting. Conversations that once felt impossible become possible again.

Because here's the heart of the matter: There is no emotionally healthy relationship without communication. Full stop. It doesn't exist.

So, if you want connection, if you want clarity, if you want to be seen and heard, you must learn how to see and hear others too.

And that starts by understanding your path, their path, and how to walk the road to connection together.

Application

In this next section, I want to challenge you to apply what you've learned.

You've identified your path. You've begun to recognize the paths of others. Now the real shift happens when you *communicate* with that knowledge in mind.

But remember: It's not just about having the tools. It's about how you use them.

The same hammer can build a cathedral or destroy a wall.

The question is, How will you use what you've learned?

PART 2

Wisdom is knowing what to do next, skill is knowing how to do it, and virtue is doing it.

—DAVID STARR JORDAN

CHAPTER 9

Off-Ramps to Communication

Let no corrupting talk come out of your mouths, but only such as is good for building up, as fits the occasion, that it may give grace to those who hear.

—EPHESIANS 4:29

"I guess I feel like no one has ever really listened to me." Sandra had tears running down her cheeks as she shared this sentiment with the group of couples that surrounded her in folding chairs, leaning in and listening intently.

We had spent the day talking about how to strengthen relationships and better connect, and Sandra was finally starting to open up to the group.

"It just always feels as though—" Just then Sandra was interrupted by the crumpling of a bag of Doritos as her husband, Doug, stood to throw away his empty chip bag and sneak out to the bathroom. As everyone looked at Doug, he apologized for his less than ninja-like exit but clearly did not grasp what had just happened.

As the door closed, it was clear that not only had the moment passed, but Sandra had now shut down as she said, "It doesn't matter. I'm not sure what I was going to say now."

It was painfully obvious that Doug had missed a chance to connect with Sandra on a deeper level. And while this was most likely unintentional on his part, the unfortunate truth is that over time, missed connections can lead to mistrust and a belief that connection is impossible.

As a therapist, I have a front-row seat to opportunities for connection that are either met or missed. I have sat countless times in front of a couple, group, or corporate team as someone teed up a perfect opportunity for connection only for it to be fumbled, whether intentionally or unintentionally.

If paths lead to connection, off-ramps lead to disconnection. They are the stops, sidetracks, and storms on the path to connection that impede progress, cause injury, or worse.

Take a moment and think about what makes you feel frustrated, hurt, or upset when communicating with someone. What is it about those experiences that leads you to feel that way? Oftentimes, the things that frustrate us most when communicating have something to do with our communication path. Off-ramps are things that take us off the path to connection.

There are several types of off-ramps, but we are going to start with the three Ds of Doom (sounds ominous, doesn't it?).

The Three Ds of Doom!

The three Ds of Doom aren't just some scary *D* words, but instead are three things I've seen hurt communication more than anything else during my time as a therapist. They are the habits and behaviors that tend to shut down or completely change the trajectory of a conversation.

It's kind of like bringing up politics at the Thanksgiving table or talking about that one time your sibling did that thing that made everyone mad. Once you bring it up, the conversation changes, and people go from being open to being guarded.

In my experience, these three Ds are frequently present in relationships that are either falling apart, toxic, or both.

Here are the three Ds of Doom:

Defensiveness
Distraction
Dismissal

Defensiveness

Defensiveness can be described as being guarded with vigor. It's like when two people are sparring for practice and then one person hits the other. The move is preemptive and more aggressive than the situation calls for. It lashes out instead of leaning in, and it shuts down future interactions.

Here's the thing about being defensive: Regardless of why you do it, it makes you the bad guy. Every single time. And the problem with being defensive is that if you do it often, eventually people become conditioned to believe that you're being defensive even when your response is reasonable.

What starts out as the way you respond to conflict can end up being generalized as encompassing your entire personality. It's kind of like those people who join CrossFit or a jiujitsu gym (guilty as charged). It's not just a hobby; it becomes their whole identity. Similarly, when you respond defensively on a regular basis, people start to expect that you will always behave this way, and they begin to brace themselves for defensiveness before it has even happened. Although this protects them, it makes it nearly impossible for others to notice when you have changed.

Knowing this, you might find yourself wondering why anyone would ever be defensive.

Here are three research-backed reasons that someone (maybe even you) might become defensive:

1. They Feel Their Self-Image Is Threatened

One of my favorite quotes says that every villain is a hero in his own mind. We all have beliefs about who we are and how we should be perceived, and when someone challenges this identity in a negative way, we tend to respond defensively because it's easier in the moment to defend ourselves than to contemplate our entire identity. While this response makes a great deal of sense, remember that no conversation demands that you rethink your identity. You get to decide what defines you.

2. They Feel a Lack of Psychological Safety

When someone feels unsafe, their first response is often to defend themselves from the threat, rather than trying to figure out what is happening.

As an example, take the tornado sirens where I live. Since I was a child, these sirens have gone off at one of two different times:

- 11:00 a.m. on a Friday once a month (to test the alarm system)
- When there is a tornado near our city

So, if it's 8:15 p.m. on a Wednesday night and the sirens go off but the sky is clear, I'm still going to my basement to shelter. It doesn't matter if it's a false alarm; I can figure that out when I'm safe.

What's challenging is that everyone experiences psychological and emotional safety differently, and so sometimes, one person can experience a threat while another person feels completely safe. It's like that second person doesn't even hear the sirens.

The unspoken variations in the way people define safety can often cause problems. For some, the very idea of a difficult conversation leads them to feel unsafe and then defensive. In that case, it's important to understand what leads the defensive person to feel the way they do so you know how to help them feel more at ease.

Pro tip: How a person experiences psychological safety is directly related to their communication path. When you know someone's path, you can better understand how to create safety for them.

3. Their Threat Response Is Activated

If a person experiences what they believe is a threat to their status, certainty, autonomy, relevance, or fairness, this can activate the same neural circuits that are activated during physical danger.[1] This by no means justifies defensiveness, but it does beg the question of what is causing the person to perceive a threat. Many times, when we answer that question, we can change the narrative, change our words, or change the environment to allow for a greater sense of safety.

In my experience, defensiveness is a primary threat to deeper connection because it communicates to others that they are engaged in a conflict rather than a discussion.

Have you seen the trend where people record videos of themselves screaming as though something is terribly wrong to see what their friends and family do? In those videos, people who are otherwise logical and rational begin screaming, not because they know what's wrong, but because the other person's behavior has told them something is wrong. Defensiveness is like this. It introduces a greater perceived risk and threat to a conversation regardless of whether it's justified.

Each of the PATHS deals with defensiveness differently:

- Peacemakers overlook it.
- Advocates call it out.
- Thinkers make a counterargument.
- Harbors entertain it with hopes to better understand.
- Sparks shut down.

One important truth about defensiveness that isn't always shared is that if you are attacking someone and they respond defensively, that's a normal response to being attacked. If you're at a baseball game and a foul ball is flying toward you and your plate of nachos, you're going to put your hands up in defense because it's the safe thing to do. It minimizes the damage. Sure, your nachos are ruined, but you escape further harm. Sometimes, people argue that you shouldn't put your hands up to stop the foul ball. They reason that if you really loved them, you'd let the ball hit you.

Just so we are clear, healthy love never asks you to do that.

If you often find yourself defensive because you are in fact being attacked, it's important to note that you are not actually being defensive. You are being protective, and the goal should be not only to protect yourself but also to prevent future attacks.

Distraction

The second D of Doom is twofold. Distraction can look like either being distracted or else distracting from the point or conversation at hand. Being distracted is unfortunately very easy since we all carry devices that steal our attention and make focusing seem unnatural. The other form of distraction takes place when someone turns a conversation toward something they would rather talk about.

Let's break both of these down further.

1. Being Distracted

This type of distraction happens when you are literally not listening or paying attention—you're not in the headspace to focus on a conversation. You may be flooded (overwhelmed), frustrated, or in your feelings. We've all been there, and if you have kids, you know what it's like to be mid-sentence when someone starts screaming, yelling, or physically interrupting a conversation.

Regardless of the reason for the distraction, the message to the person talking is "What you are saying doesn't matter" or perhaps even "You don't matter." If someone takes the time to talk to you about something they find important, your job is to either show up entirely in that conversation or else tell them you can't talk now but you'll circle back.

One easy way to avoid distraction is to literally put your

phone down or in your pocket when someone is talking to you. Rather than wrestle with temptation, set yourself up for success by eliminating potential distraction.

If you have kids who are likely to distract you, refrain from talking until you know you have some time. When my wife and I were young parents, sometimes this meant talking out on the deck or in the garage.

Remember that if the conversation matters, it matters to be present.

2. Distracting from the Point

Often a conversation begins in one place but then becomes unfocused as people take it in new directions—like outward ripples that make the conversation more complicated and take it further and further from the original point. That's distraction. And some people are experts at creating and talking about the ripples. Have you ever walked away from a conversation that was supposed to be about you and realized that somewhere along the way it became about what you weren't doing, or something else entirely?

Here are three potential reasons why you might end up distracting from the point of a conversation:

1. You are emotionally overwhelmed.

   Solution: Keep conversations under ten minutes and develop emotional regulation skills.
2. You may have ADHD or another type of neurodivergence and struggle to maintain attention.

   Solution: Own it, ask for what you need, and do what helps you stay focused.

3. It is easier than taking responsibility for something you did wrong.

   Solution: Do you know how to make a small problem a bigger problem? Deny that there is a small problem. If you are in the wrong, just say so. Distracting from the point doesn't change the problem; it only exacerbates it.

If distracting from the point of conversations is a legitimate struggle for you, it's okay to ask for a reminder of the topic at hand. Or if you are speaking and the other person is distracting from the point, it's okay to say so and ask them to return to the original topic.

For some communication paths, like Peacemaker, Harbor, or Spark, asking to return to the topic at hand can feel like a monumental ask. It can feel like asking for too much or being rude.

This makes sense, but here's a different take that might help. If the topic is important, redirecting the conversation back to the point honors the importance of the subject and honors the people in the conversation. There is strength, honor, and respect in maintaining the focus. Pointing out drift isn't rude; it's respectful.

Just say this: "I think we've lost sight of the topic at hand. Can we come back to it?"

Dismissal

If you have ever had your feelings, ideas, or opinions dismissed when you were talking about something important, you know how destructive dismissal can be.

Dismissing someone can take a variety of forms:

- Minimizing: "Are you really going to make a big deal about this?"
- Comparing: "If I asked one hundred people, all of them would agree with me."
- Intellectualizing: "I don't think that what you are saying makes sense."
- Judging: "The way you feel is overly sensitive and wrong."

If you recognize yourself in any of these examples, know that it's important to avoid this behavior. One of the greatest hurts I see in any type of relationship is the dismissal of someone's feelings. And sometimes, quite surprisingly to a client, ceasing to be dismissive changes everything even if the other person's views or feelings don't change. One of the greatest shifts you can make to stop being dismissive is to adopt this approach:

If it matters to them, it matters to me.

This is especially true if the person you are talking to happens to be your spouse, partner, family member, or colleague. Recognize that the person is not asking you if it's okay to feel the way they do, but rather, they are communicating that they feel or see things that way. You don't have to agree, but you do have to listen and demonstrate that you understand what they are saying.

If you struggle with some of these dismissive behaviors, you aren't inherently flawed or a bad person. Instead, you are a person who is developing self-awareness and improving. It takes real courage to acknowledge problems and bad habits, and this is an important step in self-improvement.

If you are reading this chapter and feeling pretty sure that everyone around you is a terrible communicator, it might be a good idea to thoughtfully consider your role in the situations at hand. Sometimes other people have such obviously bad communication habits that they steal most of the spotlight, and while this makes sense, it also may lead us to play the "it's everyone else's fault" card. While this can be a very attractive card to play, it can also stall our own growth. This can be an even greater problem for Peacemakers, who naturally seek group consensus but still retain their private opinions. Without learning how to speak up, Peacemakers may find themselves silently resentful.

While the three Ds of Doom are frequent detractors from good communication, they are not the only ones. The next sections highlight other significant inhibitors of communication.

When they show up, communication shuts down.

Lies

It probably goes without saying that lies hurt communication and relationships suffer because of them. So, rather than explain the obvious reasons for that, I'd like to explain why people lie, based on both my experience in therapy and the latest research.

1. Self-Preservation

If you have ever been confronted and felt caught off-guard, you most likely understand the temptation to lie. While it makes sense that someone might lie to avoid loss in those moments, it's when we feel we have the most to lose that we actually have the most to gain.

I see this frequently in relationships where there has been a betrayal and someone is confronted. What feels like being asked to admit bad behavior and potentially ruin a relationship is often an opportunity to lead a freer and healthier life by telling the truth. Admittedly, it rarely feels like it in the moment, but the moments in which we are most tempted to cover up our behavior are often the same ones that can save us if we are willing to be honest.

2. Social Approval

Most of us want to be liked and respected by our peers. It's human nature to want to be liked, but sometimes people feel the easiest way to garner respect is by painting a picture that looks better than the original. There are some obvious problems with this approach, like the risk of eventually being found out, but in my experience, there is an even greater problem with lying for social approval: It means no one ever sees or can help with the challenges you face. This can keep you locked in a cycle of stuckness, where you need to ask for help, but asking for help means admitting to lying. Another by-product of lying to gain social approval is that it results in profound loneliness because you are never really known. What's more, the things most people lie about, if shared, would only make them more relatable and respected. I have met many people in my work and travels, but the ones who stand out (and who I respect the most) are the ones who were honest about themselves rather than presenting an image of how they wanted me to see them.

3. Personal Gain

For some, the greatest temptation to lie comes when they want to achieve a certain goal—an outcome, advantage, or "win"—they feel like they couldn't reach without lying. Think fudging the numbers to close a deal at work, win over a date, or avoid a difficult conversation with your spouse. These types of lies are often the most destructive to relationships because they cause others to question your character in addition to your decisions. For people who struggle with this type of dishonesty, radical accountability is required and, in many cases, the willingness to stop lying even if they have not been caught. It is important to note that when this type of lying is frequent, it is often the result of childhood trauma and neglect, where someone learned over time that the only real way to get what they needed was to get it for themselves. In these cases, therapy and processing of the past will do wonders to help discontinue the lying.

If you struggle with lying, understand that changing a knee-jerk reaction such as lying is going to be difficult. Initially, the lies might still happen, but the key to changing your behavior is owning it and clarifying as soon as you realize you've lied. This might sound like "What I just said wasn't the truth. Here's what I would have liked to have said that is more accurate." This transparency will go a long way toward helping yourself and others begin to rebuild trust.

Secrets

I will never forget the fateful day when I met with a client who had been referred to me by a mutual friend. The client was a successful tech entrepreneur who was well known in his industry. The initial session was much like any other intake session, and we talked about all the usual things, including what was going well and what wasn't. What was unique was that this client appeared to have everything together. He was immaculately dressed, smelled amazing, and said all the right things. In fact, the client said so many "right" things that I began to feel a little bit like he was running for office. This led me to ask, "Is there anything you're holding back?"

My client slowly nodded, and after an uncomfortable silence, he said, "I am. But I don't want to talk about it right now." I told him that I understood, and said that secrets hold a great deal of power over us and that it was important for him to trust me before sharing his. My client explained that he had felt conflicted for some time about whether to share his secret and would consider discussing it at another time.

I nodded my head and told him that I understood but would also like to challenge him if he was willing. He said yes, and I explained that secrets can seem a long way away from our daily life, so sometimes we need to remind ourselves that they are always with us.

I asked my client to stop on his way to the parking lot outside my office building and pick up a tiny pebble from the landscaping. This pebble would represent his secret. I told him to put it in his shoe each morning and pray about what to do with the secret. I watched my client go from willing to hesitant before he said, "But I have really expensive shoes." He wasn't wrong. I had been admiring his shoes, which appeared to have cost as much as my mortgage payment, since he walked in. I acknowledged his concern and reassured him that it was up to him to decide whether he wanted to follow my plan or not. The client left, and I was certain that I had gone too far.

A pebble in his shoe? What was I thinking? I braced myself for the inevitable disappearance of this client and wondered if I would get hate mail from the Society for Expensive Italian Shoes. Weeks passed, but then one day I received a phone call. The client wanted to meet again. We set up a time and, in my head, I vowed to do things differently. No more shoe talk, and no more pebbles.

My client could keep his secret as long as he wanted.

When the time of our appointment arrived, I was sitting at my desk looking out my third-floor windows, as I often do, writing sticky notes of ideas for future books. When my client came in, I turned and was caught off guard by how pale he looked. Without saying a word, he walked over to my desk, looked at me with tears running down his face, and leaned down to take a tiny pebble from his shoe.

He dropped the pebble on my desk, and it bounced three times—*tick, tick, tick*—as my client looked at me and said, "I'm tired."

It would be nice to be able to tell you that everything changed that day for my client. Things did change, but it took some time, and the result was different from what he expected. But what happened was transformational, and it started with an admission: "I'm tired."

I am convinced that secrets are the carbon monoxide of relationships. They blend into the background but can kill us over time. And the longer we keep them to ourselves, the more harm they cause. If you have a secret, the only way to take away its power is to tell someone. While this requires effort, so does holding on to something toxic.

Reflect

Each PATHS style will have different areas of susceptibility to communication off-ramps. The goal is to know what to look out for.

Here are some off-ramps that might apply to each style:

- Peacemaker: Avoids conflict.
- Advocate: Can be confrontational.
- Thinker: Can be dismissive or emotionally detached.
- Harbor: Can be indirect or vague.
- Spark: May overreact or dramatize situations.

Now ask yourself the following questions:

1. What stood out to me most in this chapter? Why?
2. What do I need to spend some time working on? What is one small step I can take today to improve?
3. Knowing my communication style, which of these areas am I most likely to struggle in?
4. Where do I have opportunity for growth?

CHAPTER 10

On-Ramps to Communication

One of the easiest things to do is to point out what not to do. Much of what we see on social media and in other places is aimed at pointing out problems rather than finding solutions. And while this is certainly understandable and usually gets the most attention, I often find myself faced with clients who are experts on what not to do but are still wondering what they are supposed to do instead.

This chapter focuses on what to do if you want to build connection with someone. Regardless of our PATHS style, we all want to connect in deep and meaningful ways. Some styles will have an easier time with certain methods than others. This doesn't mean one style is better than another; the goal is to understand your PATHS style and where you might develop new skills.

If you want thriving personal and professional relationships, what follows are communication on-ramps—or opportunities for connection—that you can practice to build healthy and lasting relationships.

Empathy

Empathy is generally defined as the capacity to recognize, understand, and feel what another person is experiencing from their frame of reference.[1]

You may have heard it described as "walking a mile in someone else's shoes," or as Brené Brown defines it: "communicating that incredibly healing message of 'You're not alone.'"[2]

Regardless of the definition you use, empathy is one of the most impactful ways to connect with someone, though it is something many people struggle to understand.

Theresa Wiseman has done a great deal of research on empathy and states that there are four primary attributes of empathy:

1. **Perspective taking.** This requires you to put your views and perspective to the side in order to consider someone else's. It transcends agreement or disagreement and instead is about seeing the world how the other person sees it rather than from your own perspective.
2. **Staying out of judgment.** Judgment kills deep communication. It's like realizing that someone is keeping score when you thought you were just playing for fun. Or it's like that feeling you have when you are being silly and someone pulls out their phone to record you. It stops you in your tracks.
3. **Recognizing emotion in other people.** This requires you to recognize emotion in yourself. It is challenging

to recognize emotions in others that we do not notice in ourselves.

4. **Communicating that emotion.** This is demonstrating to the other person that you understand how they feel.[3]

It's important to understand that different PATHS styles will have different challenges. The places where you struggle are opportunities for growth, not avoidance.

If you struggle with empathy, spend some time learning more about how Harbors approach communication, and watch your capacity for empathy soar.

While I love Wiseman's framework as a great general guide, many of my clients still struggled with how to show up well in a relationship when empathy was needed. In response, I developed my own framework for empathy.

My framework is an acronym, LISTEN, which highlights the first and most important thing to remember if you really want to communicate and connect with someone. In fact, I would argue that simply listening will get you a long way in terms of connection, no matter your communication type. The reason is that listening well is really challenging to do—and so is finding someone to listen to us. How often do you find someone who is willing to just listen, without an agenda or interruption? It is rare. If you are this person to others, thank you. My advice would be to find a person who does this for you too. We all deserve to have a person in our life who listens, and if you are in a serious romantic relationship, it should be a minimum requirement for that relationship.

Here's my unique spin on empathy using the LISTEN framework:

L—Look Beneath the Surface

Emotions aren't always obvious; pay attention to what's unsaid. In many cases, what is unsaid is what needs to be discussed. Also, be aware of the feelings you experience while the other person is talking. Your feelings are often a clue as to what to focus on or what about the conversation matters most to you. The best communicators speak to what is beneath the surface rather than just what is said aloud. This requires you to be able to notice your own emotions and communicate them. If you struggle with this, journaling can help.

Ask: "I notice you seem distant. What's on your heart?"

I—Initiate Questions

Don't assume—ask open-ended questions. An open-ended question creates opportunity for many different answers while a closed question can simply be answered yes or no and doesn't inspire further conversation. Although we are often told not to make assumptions, it can be hard to avoid—especially if we have been in a relationship for a long time.

This is because our brains keep track of patterns and themes in order to operate efficiently. Thinkers especially tend to notice patterns as well as inconsistencies. While the conclusions they draw often make sense, the problem is that if they aren't careful, Thinkers can rely solely on their own information to decide instead of collecting new information like a Peacemaker might. To avoid this tendency, Thinkers can challenge themselves to get curious for the purpose of verifying their position rather than defending it.

Imagine you're watching *Wheel of Fortune* when a puzzle has one letter left, and your brain is practically shouting out that it knows the answer! It's kind of like the time in 2024 when contestant Will Jordan was faced with what many thought was an obvious answer. While most people correctly thought the answer was "Give yourself a round of applause," Will mistakenly guessed "Treat yourself a round of sausage." Close, but not quite.

Looking at the same puzzle and same empty squares, Will's brain came up with a wildly different guess from what most expected. What seemed likely to him based on his knowledge, experiences, and education was much different from the norm. In relationships, your brain often tries to figure out what the other person is going to think or say based on past experiences, but it doesn't always guess correctly.

One of the biggest challenges in long-term relationships is learning to bypass assumptions and be curious instead. When we adopt a sense of curiosity, people feel listened to and deeply connected. But remember that curiosity is different from asking questions to prove something or push an agenda. When asking questions, think less *Law and Order* and more intrigued seven-year-old (but without the frequency).

Say: "I don't want to guess or get this wrong. Can you share what's weighing on you?"

S—See Them

Your job isn't to fix the other person—it's to see them. This is going to be particularly hard for some people to hear, but most of the time when someone shares something vulnerable or deep, they do not want you to fix their feelings. Instead, they are simply wanting to be heard.

This is critically important to understand if you want to communicate with empathy. And, not to point fingers, but men often struggle the most with this. Our knee-jerk reaction is usually to assess and fix any negative feelings or problems, but in the process, we often end up "fixing" someone who just wanted to be seen. If this is something you struggle with, understand that although you likely have the best of intentions, it's not usually experienced that way. So, if you're going into a tough conversation, know that you may need to avoid your first instinctive response to the other person's pain. Instead of rushing to solutions, suspend your judgment and listen.

Say: "I can see why this is painful for you. You don't have to go through this alone."

T—Take Their Perspective

Empathy isn't agreement—it's understanding. Think of it this way: Taking another person's perspective isn't about whether you agree with them; it's about seeing a situation from the same angle they're seeing it from. Harbors are naturally good at this because they can intuitively sense and respond to feelings, both spoken and unspoken. The secret to doing this well is to find a way to make the person speaking to you your primary focus.

When I am sitting with a client, I do this by imagining that the person sitting in front of me is a pastry chef who is telling me all about something they baked. I imagine that it's my job to understand the recipe and their baking process. Only then can I begin to understand how the results turned out the way they did. Sometimes what seems like a poorly made cake looks different when you learn that the baker didn't have the right ingredients, burned their hand on the oven, and had to rush the mixture.

Similarly, some of the most incredible things that have happened in the world probably looked uneventful to people who were watching from a different angle.

Our perspective is personal and impacts not only how we see ourselves but also how we see others. Healthy communication isn't about having a winning perspective, but instead about having a *willing* perspective. When we are willing to hear a different perspective, connection deepens.

Early in my career, I had the opportunity to train with Terry Real, a talented and well-known therapist, when he hosted an event in Minneapolis.

During this event, I watched—along with fifty-plus other therapists—as Terry worked with one couple at a time. After each session, Terry would have the couple step out of the room and the therapists would discuss the model Terry had created and ask questions about his approach.

Everyone in the room was a therapist or therapist in training, so it's safe to say that many of us had a high degree of communication experience. But here's what fascinated me: Without fail, there would always be one or more people who felt that Terry had missed the point of what someone said.

Inevitably, someone would raise their hand and ask some version of "Why did you spend the whole session talking about *x* when you should have been talking about *y*?"

But here's the thing—they weren't wrong, and neither was Terry. If you are communicating to connect, the only wrong move is to refuse to see another person's perspective.

Wanting to connect means acknowledging and recognizing other PATHS even if they aren't your preferred style. You'd be amazed at how much you can grow your sense of connection with others simply by owning that other PATHS exist.

Say: "If I were in your position, I'd probably feel this way too. I'm sorry for the pain you are feeling."

E—Express Validation

It's critical to acknowledge others' emotions before trying to repair them. Say: "Your feelings are real, and they matter. I see you." Remember when we talked about people who grew up in families where they couldn't talk about their emotions? These people may have been told that they were "too much" or "too emotional"—and these same people grow into adults who desperately want to be able to talk about their emotions and be heard. When they feel they've been seen and heard, they are willing to listen to how you think. But not until then.

Many people overlook the value of validation. It's not just a buzzword or therapy trick, but a reality that changes hearts and minds. When you acknowledge the value of someone's feelings, you unlock vulnerability that would not be accessible otherwise.

But many people get stuck believing that validation equals agreement. It does not. Feelings are much like art (which is why art evokes emotion). When you look at a painting, you might think "I like this" or "I don't like it," but you would never refuse to acknowledge the existence of the painting. Nor would you deny the effort it took to make the painting and the colors of paint used. Validating someone's feelings is like acknowledging the painting, even if it's not to your taste.

Ask: "What would help you feel more supported in this moment?"

N—Nurture Connection

Trust and connection are built through small, consistent moments over time.

Think of relationships and connection like a bonsai tree. Bonsai trees are known for their beauty and for what they represent. But did you know that the type of bonsai tree most people envision is typically at least ten to fifty years old? Bonsai trees take at least a decade to develop a well-established trunk, roots, and branch structure.

Relationships aren't much different. A beautiful relationship isn't the result of one conversation, but instead a commitment to ongoing communication and care.

Many clients come to my office in a desperate attempt to quickly make up for months (or sometimes years) of neglecting a relationship. It's as if they wake up one day and realize that they have forgotten to care for the relationship, and then expect that if they pour some extra effort into it that day it will make all the difference.

Unfortunately, nurturing a relationship is a lot like growing compound interest. It requires consistent effort and time. When some people hear this they immediately bristle and wonder what nurturing a relationship might require, but the truth is that for many relationships, the time investment is much lower than you might think.

Research tells us that to have a healthy primary relationship, you must spend about seven hours a week together.[4] This means that out of the 168 hours in a week, you must give the person you are most connected with 4 percent to have a great relationship. Friendships require even less time, but it's important to note that any relationship you want to thrive is going to require you to invest some time and energy.

Here are three impactful ways to nurture a relationship:

1. Ask well-constructed open-ended questions. People love to talk about themselves, and a heartfelt question from

someone who genuinely cares will make most people swoon. Remember to stick around for the answer and to ditch any agenda you might have. Ask questions because you want to know the person better, and then consider the answer.

2. Focus on what feels most nurturing to the other person. For some friends it's a text, for others it's a call, and for still others it might be a video message. Regardless, invest time in understanding what the other person values most, and then spend your time there.
3. Provide value. This might sound a bit like sales advice, but it's true in personal relationships as well. Relationships that thrive are the ones that make each person better for being in the relationship. Share articles, thoughts, and information related to the other person's interests. Serving others and helping them with the things that matter to them is what grows a relationship the fastest.

Going Deep

"Friends, do I have permission to go deep with you?"

This is how I start many of my keynote talks, because I've learned over time that if you give people a choice to go somewhere meaningful with you, most will.

Most people love to talk with people who go deep. You know, those people who, instead of asking you about the weather, end up talking with you about that dream you have but are afraid to go after. Because when you have these types of conversations, you share what matters most—and, if the other person receives those things well, intimacy is formed and relationships are built.

If you have never had this type of relationship, the first time can be eye-opening.

Thankfully, I have many therapist friends and thinkers who also value going deep and are willing to do so often. I cannot tell you how many times I have met someone at a conference or event and ended up talking for a long time for this reason. Once you know the value of going deep, you realize it's where all the best relationship things happen. I think this was a gift that Jesus had. There is no place in the Bible that mentions Jesus speaking to someone about the weather, sports, or anything else that was shallow. Instead, Jesus made his words count.

Imagine if you had a limit on the number of words you could speak each day. What would you choose to use them on? What conversations would you want to have, or what questions would you want to ask the people you care about most?

With this perspective, consider that the art to deep conversation comes down to three things:

1. Create a safe enough environment to go deep. Many people struggle because they immediately attempt to ask a question that is well outside the degree of safety that has been established.

   Consider this example. When I was introduced to someone at an event, I shook their hand and told them my name. Without skipping a beat they looked at me and asked, "What would you tell your younger self if you could go back in time?" Although it's a great question, the reality is that without a name tag, I couldn't even remember this person's name. It was a little early for us to be talking about what we'd tell our younger selves. There was no safety established in our relationship and no reason for me to want to be vulnerable with a stranger.

I've seen a similar phenomenon with people who have been to therapy, briefly picked up a concept there, and then attempted to use it when dating. This can work against them, because most people are repelled by questions that go too deep too fast. Safety comes from small questions that go increasingly deeper each time.

2. Give people time to answer. If you are going to ask a big question, make sure you're willing to stick around for the answer. When I played chess regularly, I would sometimes play with players who took a long time to respond. I would move a piece in three seconds, and they would take thirty seconds to move theirs. Every second felt like too long to wait. And yet that's the time it took. So, if we're going to have a meaningful conversation and we're going to ask the question, we need to give space for them to answer. For many people, the answer is going to take time, and that's okay. We all have our different rhythms and pace.
3. Find the right time and place. Our goal should be to read the room and identify what is appropriate in the moment. Not every conversation is a place for deep connection. Some relationships are shallow and temporary, and that's okay. One of the keys to knowing if you should go deep with someone is knowing if you trust them with your stuff. Are you willing to be vulnerable with them? If not, recognize that while depth might be a future goal, the relationship cannot sustain it today. Sometimes you must

craft the message needed in the moment, not the one you most want to give.

When you are speaking with someone, whether you're using the LISTEN framework, going deep, or otherwise, the questions to ask yourself are:

1. Do I want this conversation to continue?
2. If I do, am I making it easy for the other person to speak to me?

Number two is key. If you want to talk with someone but you make it difficult for them to speak to you, or are unwilling to be present, they won't engage. People have many choices of how to spend their time and many things vying for their attention. If you want to talk with someone, you have to make it easier for them to talk to you than to do something else.

I am often reminded of this on airplanes. In the past—before the internet, in-flight television, and cell phones—people had to simply sit in their seat and decide between talking with the person next to them or reading a book. Those were the choices. "Is this person more interesting than *War and Peace*?" But today that's not the case.

Today, if you want to talk with the person next to you on a plane, you have some competition. I think this is a good thing, but it means you need to up your game to be more interesting than old episodes of *The Office*. In our house, that's a pretty high bar to overcome.

So, remember as you go out into the world that the best

on-ramp to communication will always be being a person who makes it easy for others to talk to them.

Reflect

Hands-down the best on-ramp to connection is when you meet someone else on their communication path. Consider for a moment the people who are closest to you. What paths are they on, and how could you communicate with them in a more connection-building and meaningful way today?

Answer these questions:

1. Is there a relationship in your life that needs more care? What can you do today to nurture it?
2. Think of a time when someone showed you empathy. How can you give that gift to someone else today?
3. Which of the communication on-ramps is easiest for you? Which one is most difficult?

Don't just think about doing the next right thing—do it.

CHAPTER 11

Conflict

When people learn that I am a therapist, the thing I probably get asked about most is how to do conflict well. I've been asked in planes, trains, taxicabs, and many other places. And as someone who spent most of his early life running away from conflict, it feels a bit surreal for me to now be offering advice to people I've just met. I understand why they ask, though. Not so long ago I would have done the very same thing.

In my experience, most people fall into one of two categories: They either like conflict or they run from it, and there seems to be little room in the middle.

I faced this immediately when I began working in the prison system shortly after graduate school. As a chronic "yes" person, I rarely found myself embroiled in any kind of conflict. In fact, when it came to conflict, I had mastered the art of maneuvering my way out of conflict in a way that left me a little dignity and also allowed me to skip all confrontation. While this had worked swimmingly with colleagues and friends, it fell short when I worked in the prison system because "yes" carried a lot more weight there. In prison, failing to address the elephant in the room meant that people could get hurt and change would not happen. And so, I did what any therapist would do when they realized they needed to change: I buttoned up my cardigan, made sure my fountain pen had enough ink, and journaled about my feelings—and then entered the world to face the conflict.

Maybe it was a bit less dramatic than that. Early on I did what many people do when they suddenly realize they can't continue to avoid conflict. A common reaction is to decide that every opportunity for conflict should now be taken and engaged. And while I can understand this reaction (I did it too), what ends up happening is that we find our otherwise conflict-avoidant selves engaging in lots of unnecessary conflict. When we do this, it can be easy to feel beat-up, misunderstood, and overwhelmed (which are all the things we were trying to avoid in the first place). What's more, knowing how to initiate conflict doesn't mean we know how to resolve it.

Some people are great at starting conflict but haven't figured out the working-through-it part yet. Others can resolve conflicts but are so good at being content that they never bring up a conflict to resolve.

Before you go engaging in conflict with the next person you meet, let's talk about some fundamental aspects of conflict and how to identify, approach, and resolve it well.

Conflict vs. Fighting

Conflict can be defined as "a perceived incompatibility of actions, goals, or ideas."[1]

Fighting, on the other hand, often involves a defensive or aggressive reaction to a perceived threat, rejection, or unmet needs, and is usually marked by raised emotions, blame, or withdrawal.

Conflict often implies wanting to resolve or repair, while fighting often means wanting to destroy. Or, put another way, fighting is what happens when conflict becomes combative.

When you view conflict through the PATHS model, you can see that your ability to work through conflict will be limited to how fluent you are in other communication styles. If you cannot or refuse to adjust to different styles, you will end up stuck in either conflict or conflict avoidance.

By nature, conflict is meant to lead toward resolution and repair. Its purpose is to address, correct, and improve—which many of us were never taught.

Think back to your childhood. Did your parents have conflict, or did they fight? My experience was fighting, not conflict. And this isn't the part of the book where I try to get you to be upset with your parents. Instead, I want you to consider what you were taught about conflict. Many of us never learned that conflict is a tool that can be used to correct and even bring people closer. If you have only ever experienced fighting, it's easy to think conflict is like a nuclear weapon that, once detonated, destroys everything in its path.

But healthy conflict isn't fighting; it's working through a disagreement in a way that leaves you feeling better for having had it, even if you don't look forward to having another one. When you realize this, you begin to experience a sense of empowerment about conflict that many people miss.

Conflict is neither good nor bad; it's simply part of healthy communication.

Here are some reminders about conflict for each PATHS style:

- Peacemaker: You can have conflict and tension and still be liked.
- Advocate: Working together through conflict strengthens relationships.
- Thinker: Opening yourself to new perspectives helps you to think more effectively.
- Harbor: The deepest relationships are the ones that can accommodate emotions and work through conflict.
- Spark: It's worth slowing down to work through conflict.

Keep these things in mind as we discuss how to do conflict well.

The Wants and Needs Framework

To do conflict well, you must lead with the need.

After working with hundreds of couples, I have learned several frameworks for navigating conflict from notable and amazing therapists, psychologists, and coaches. I have tried all of them, and while many work very well, the problem I kept running into was that it's difficult to remember a complicated framework in the moment a conflict arises. I don't know if you can relate, but when I find myself in conflict, my thoughts often feel so disorganized that I'm hardly able to remember my name—so a multistep conflict framework is the last thing on my mind. Instead of relying on a framework that probably won't be remembered at the moment it needs to be remembered the most, I came up with one that is simple, direct, and effective.

The Problem

Before entering any conflict, our first goal should be to understand what the conflict is about. While this seems rudimentary, many people struggle to even agree on what the problem is. When there is no agreement on the problem, there will not be agreement on a solution. This is made worse when conflict is entered into impulsively or reactively because, when that happens, most people are trying to express a feeling rather than resolve a conflict.

Here are some guidelines for defining the problem at the heart of a conflict. The problem should be specific and able to be expressed in one or two sentences. If the problem cannot be explained in just a couple sentences, there is a good chance that the conflict is about more than one problem. And while sometimes that feels necessary, the reality is that it's difficult enough to resolve one problem, let alone several all at once. So we must practice getting good at identifying and defining the actual problem, rather than jumbling up five issues at once and attempting to sort everything out.

Defining a problem also makes it possible for it to be solved because it creates agreement about what the problem is. It allows people to see the problem as something they are both facing and working to resolve together. When there is no consensus on the problem itself, there is little hope of resolution—and it can be easy to see the other person as the problem instead.

When you have identified and defined the problem, it is important to make sure the other person both understands how you are defining it and is willing to attempt to resolve that specific problem. If they do not understand the problem or need to ask questions, it's important to allow them to do so. I cannot tell you how many times I have witnessed couples escalate from conflict to fighting because they do not have a shared understanding of the problem at hand.

The Want

The want is what you *want* to have happen—the ideal outcome you would hope for when entering the conflict. It's like getting the exact birthday gift you asked for or that day when pumpkin spice lattes come out; it's the best thing that could happen in that circumstance. It's also not always the thing you get. The point of naming the want is that it teaches you to identify and communicate what you want, which is something many people struggle with.

Before you say that you don't *know* what you want, I'm here to tell you that's okay. Unfortunately, many people struggle to identify what they want, and even fewer have ever been asked. If that's been your experience, I'm sorry.

The fantastic news is that as an adult, you get to ask for what you want. This is true even if you don't immediately know what you want. For many people, naming the want is challenging, and it's also something they need to practice asking for. Along the way, know that what you think you want will not always be accurate, and that's okay. As you develop greater self-awareness and insight, what you want will come to you with a greater degree of clarity.

It's worth noting that even if you can communicate a specific want, not all wants will be met. A want is not a need and is therefore something to aim for but not required.

Let's talk about what *is* required to resolve conflict: meeting a need.

The Need

The need is the aspect of a conflict that matters most in terms of resolution and repair. It's the minimum result that you are willing to walk away with and still feel the matter has been resolved. It's probably not the exact outcome that you would hope for, but it's enough for you to feel like you can move on. For some, the need feels even more daunting to determine than the want, but here's an easy way to identify the need: It's the thing you'll be bitter and resentful about if you don't get it. Maybe it's an apology, validation, or simply to be heard, but it's the thing that matters most, and is probably connected to an area where you feel deeply hurt.

Identifying and naming needs can be painful, because for many people growing up, they knew their wants were luxuries, but even having their basic needs met may have been questionable. If this has been your story, it deserves attention and grieving, because we all have needs that must be met, regardless of whether the people in our lives have met them. Peacemakers, Harbors, and Sparks may especially struggle with sharing their needs, all for different but legitimate reasons. Knowing this, people with those communication paths may have to practice asking for what they need with Thinkers and Advocates who are more comfortable asking for and fulfilling needs.

Identifying and asking for our needs is an opportunity for growth and something we often must learn by trial and error. The good news is that when you know what you need and ask for it, you will discover who really values you, because your needs will matter to them.

The Setup

The best way to use the wants and needs framework is to think through it before you initiate a conflict, ensuring that the conflict is not reactive, but rather intentional and about something you've decided is worth discussing. This requires you to pause before entering conflict, which often seems shocking to people. But doing this on the front end of a conflict usually makes the conflict easier to resolve as a result. Over time, many of my clients have integrated this approach into their relationships, and the pausing part takes very little time. In fact, clients often report that after a few times of using the model, they end up being able to skip the conflict because when they identify and communicate what they want and need, the other person usually just meets them there. This is the goal. But when you're just getting started, recognize and give yourself grace that you will most likely need to write out your wants and needs. Remember that you are learning a new skill, and it takes practice. Be patient and know that if both parties are willing, change will occur.

Here's a common question about the framework: "What if my want and need are the same?" Great question! In this case, either you only have a need, which is okay sometimes, or else you aren't truly considering the question. The want would add something positive to the relationship, whereas the need simply keeps it going. The want can be difficult to identify and discuss if you struggle with vulnerability, because it's something you probably wouldn't normally say. The reason to say it is to give the person you're talking to an opportunity to show up in a deeper way to build the relationship. Think of the want like dessert. Everyone wants it, but no one needs it. But who doesn't love getting dessert?

When you approach the other person to talk, it's important to understand that while they may agree on the problem, they might have a want or need as well. They should be encouraged to ask for what they want and need too, because when you both get what you need, the relationship can keep moving forward.

Rocks and Ripples

Did you know that the Guinness World Record for the most consecutive skips of a stone on water is eighty-eight times and was achieved by Kurt Steiner on September 6, 2013, in the Allegheny National Forest in Pennsylvania?[2]

This impressive feat beautifully illustrates a phenomenon I often observe when clients engage in conflict.

"Skipping," as I call it, occurs when a conflict jumps from problem to problem, eventually landing at a point far from where the conflict started.

Perhaps you can relate to the following situation. A couple sits down on my couch, and they begin to tell me about a recent conflict. The initial conflict they describe is often a simple one; maybe one of them said something hurtful or failed to complete a task. It usually seems like an easy enough conflict to resolve—but then come the skips.

Frequently, conflict begins with a "rock"—the issue that causes the initial splash. It's the catalyst for the conflict, the problem that needs to be resolved. However, when the conflict isn't handled well, the rock skips to another point, and then another.

In my experience, these skips often follow a predictable pattern and order:

Skip 1: Adjacent Arguments

A conflict might begin with the familiar "You forgot to grab the garbage can" but soon become not only about the garbage but also about the mail that was dropped in a puddle earlier in the day. People often use adjacent arguments to justify their emotions or support the validity of an argument. An adjacent argument is the beginning of case building and most often happens when a person feels they do not have a voice unless they are willing to fight to be heard. These arguments indicate a more serious problem, which is that past conflicts are not being resolved.

Skip 2: Historical and Unresolved Arguments

These arguments are like burrs that stick to anything; they are sure to keep conflict going. They are the big brothers and big sisters to adjacent arguments, as they illustrate that not only is there a problem today, but there has been a problem for a long time. What's interesting about historical arguments and the retelling of past issues is that humans are terrible eyewitnesses. In fact, we are so bad that research says we cannot be trusted to remember something a week after it happened. However, despite this knowledge, we still sometimes find ourselves engaging in this type of escalation, especially when making an adjacent argument didn't work. Building on the example about the garbage, a historical argument might sound like "Every week for the last three months I've had to fight with you to take out the trash!" or "This has been an issue for our whole relationship."

Historical arguments are tough to navigate because they often cannot be proven, but they are powder kegs waiting to explode. People use historical arguments when they believe things can't, won't, or don't change. They are the cry of someone who has lost or is losing hope.

Skip 3: Character Arguments

These arguments are the last stop on the road to a blowup and are about the character of the other person involved in the conflict. They are the nuclear option, and once the button is pressed, it is hard to come back. To build on our example, these arguments sound like "You don't take the trash out because you're lazy" or "I knew you were the type of person who wouldn't pull their weight!"

The problem with character arguments is that they're almost guaranteed to start a new argument, because when our character is attacked, we get defensive (even if the other person has a point). The conflict becomes about whether the person who forgot to take out the trash is lazy, and for most people, their knee-jerk reaction is going to be to fight. This makes sense but also illustrates why people can get so stuck in conflict—because if the solution requires someone to admit that they're lazy, the conflict is unlikely to be resolved.

When side arguments begin, it's important to redirect the conversation back to the origin of the conflict, and if you are unable to, it's good to take a break.

If you find yourself frequently having conflicts that escalate into historical and character arguments, this is a sign that you need some professional help to get back on track. This is nothing to be ashamed about, and is instead an opportunity to have a healthier relationship.

Letting Things Go

I'd be remiss if I didn't say the least popular thing before the end of the chapter.

Here it is: If you value a relationship and believe that the other person is for you, then you probably need to raise the bar on what you see as conflict-worthy.

This doesn't mean you should take abuse or be mistreated. It means that if you are in a relationship with someone who you believe generally has your best interest at heart, simply letting some things go without starting a conflict is healthy.

Conflict, even when navigated well, is often still stressful and difficult. Even though the wants and needs framework makes it easier, very few people actually enjoy conflict.

Think of your relationship like a road trip to an amazing destination, and every time you have conflict it means you need to pull off the road. While some stops are completely necessary and justified, you may not need to stop as much as you might have guessed.

For that reason, you need to be choosy about what deserves airtime in your relationship. Is it the garbage? Maybe not the first three times, though the fourth might require some discussion.

I'm not here to prescribe your standards, but I can tell you that people sometimes focus more on what they are upset about than on what's working, and, in a healthy relationship where both parties generally have good intentions and care for each other, conflict is a risky pastime. Famed clinical psychologist and relationship researcher John Gottman has found that nearly 69 percent of the problems in a typical relationship are perpetual, meaning they are ongoing and rooted in personality differences and preferences.[3] This means that some issues can be discussed but may never be fully resolved. And that's okay.

A surefire way to decide if you need to engage in conflict is to ask yourself, "Will I be upset about this tomorrow?" If the answer is yes, say something. If the answer is no, drop it. If the answer is maybe, sleep on it and see.

Remember, not every problem requires you to address it. Wield the sword of conflict only when necessary, and be intentional.

Reflect

1. What is your primary struggle with conflict? What is one thing you can apply from this chapter to improve?
2. Which is more difficult for you to identify: when to have conflict, or your wants and needs?
3. How does your PATHS style factor into conflict?
4. Do you notice a common theme in the conflicts you have?
5. Which PATHS style is most difficult for you to work through conflict with?

CHAPTER 12

Saying Hard Things

One of the best parts of my job as a therapist is getting to give people permission to have hard conversations. I define hard conversations as conversations that require you to be intentional, thoughtful, and present.

Here are a few examples of hard things to say: *I'm hurt, I have a boundary, I need something, I have an opinion, I'm scared, I've messed up, NO.*

I don't know about you, but I spent much of my life running from hard conversations.

This wasn't part of some strategy or master plan, but instead was a reaction to hurts I'd experienced. Experience had taught me that the best thing that could happen during a difficult conversation was that the other person said nothing, and the worst thing that could happen was the end of a relationship. It never occurred to me that I could say something challenging to someone and they might go so far as to validate or empathize with me.

Can you relate?

In fact, I was so good at running from difficult conversations that I literally took up running as a way to avoid difficult conversations. Early on in my marriage, when I had something to say that I was anxious about or felt could lead to conflict, I would often try to avoid the conversation by running instead. While this was great for my waistline, it also meant that I spent a lot of time running when I should have been talking. Although it sounds ridiculous now, back then I hoped that if I ran far enough I wouldn't feel the way I did, so I wouldn't have to talk about it at all. And so, mile after mile I ran, hoping the need for the conversation would go away the farther I got from home.

Maybe you've never put on running shoes to avoid a conversation, but you might still relate to the feeling of wanting to do anything other than have the talk you know you need to have.

Running from hard conversations might look like:

1. Being unavailable, whether this means being physically absent, distracted, emotionally unavailable, or stoic.
2. Overtalking, overexplaining, or highlighting anything other than what needs to be discussed.
3. Placating, pushing away, or promising to deal with things at a later time but never following through.

Have you experienced any of these in a relationship?

If you have, you know how frustrating and hurtful it can be to feel like you need to talk or trick someone into communicating with you.

Or if you are the one who tends to avoid hard conversations, consider the following question:

When did you first begin to feel like it was easier to avoid hard conversations than to have them?

The answer will tell you a lot about how you see difficult conversations today.

For me, it was shortly after my parents decided to get divorced. I was crushed by their decision and couldn't understand why they would do such a thing to our family. Not long after they divorced, I shared with them what was on my eight-year-old heart, hoping it would change their decision. When it didn't, I remember feeling like the situation was hopeless: Nothing I could say would change anything, so it would be easier to say nothing. Today, I know a lot of things my eight-year-old self didn't know about parenting and marriage, so I understand that it wasn't my responsibility to save my parents' marriage, and also that there really wasn't anything I could have said or done to change their decision. And while their divorce was a loss that I grieve, I see it much differently today.

I tell you all of this because sometimes our reluctance to talk about hard things stems from situations in our past that taught us there was little point in having the types of conversations that we now avoid. And while that may have been true for some situations, the hope is that today's circumstances—and you—are different.

Who's in Your Circle of Vulnerability?

When approaching hard conversations, one of the first things to consider is who to be vulnerable with, and the answer is: not everyone. Not everyone needs, deserves, or is interested in access to your innermost feelings and world.

Increasingly it seems like we live in a world where people can choose to either follow or unfollow us in real life, and as a result, much of our communication centers around keeping them as followers. While this might be how social media works, it doesn't lead to healthy or fulfilling relationships in the real world. It's important to recognize that you can't be all things to all people. You just can't. And so, the following sections focus on how to speak with the people in your life who are good stewards of your vulnerability and who want a relationship with you.

Bridge the Gap

If you are about to offer constructive criticism or feedback to someone you care about, their initial response will probably be one of hurt. Even if your statements are accurate, few people respond to criticism or challenge with a smile, especially if that criticism or challenge is offered in a way that falls outside the person's PATHS style. So, give the person you are talking to time and space to receive the information for the first time. If they have an immediate bad reaction, it's worth asking if they would like to have some time before they respond.

I see this pattern quite often in couples therapy and even within top leadership teams at Fortune 100 companies. Someone waits for a long time to say something they find difficult to say, and then when they finally do say it and the other person has a less than favorable response, they quickly judge the other person for being upset—when they themselves have already been upset and had time to process. Don't do that. It's important to address problems before they grow huge, but to do that you need a plan.

I chose the BRIDGE acronym for this plan, because the goal is to bridge the gap between you and the other person. No matter your communication type, you can benefit from considering not only your PATHS type, but the other person's as well. Knowing both gives you the information you need to speak the truth in a way that will truly resonate.

B—Breathe. Seems natural, right? Did you know that your breathing helps regulate your nervous system and that a calm nervous system allows you to approach conversations differently?

R—Remember the purpose and objectives of the conversation. In short, why are you having this conversation? If you don't know, the chances are that the other person doesn't either.

I—"I." Use "I" statements instead of "you" statements. "I" communicates to the other person that you're describing your own feelings and allows them to make a decision about their role in your feelings; "you" statements, on the other hand, tend to assign blame.

D—Define what you are hoping to get out of the conversation in a simple and clear manner.

G—Grace. Give grace to the other person and to yourself. Difficult conversations can carry a lot of weight, and remembering to give grace makes the conversations easier.

E—Explore next steps and eliminate confusion. Confusion is the enemy of connection. Summarize what has been said and what will happen next, whether that's another conversation later, a task, or simply stating how you feel. Make sure both of you understand and agree on the plan.

If you value a relationship, then communicating your desire to both continue and improve the relationship is often the secret sauce of having hard conversations. This is because if someone is told something difficult without any incentive—like the promise of a future healthier relationship—they are unlikely to receive it well. To state the point differently, how many days would you be willing to diet if you knew that you wouldn't lose any weight? So when you tell someone something challenging, if you want the relationship to continue, it's important to say so. Don't leave the other person guessing. Make it known that what you are asking for is an invitation to a better relationship. This simple shift from treating hard conversations as punishments to treating them like an invitation often makes all the difference.

Boundaries

Boundaries have gotten a bad rap lately. And in fairness, I can see why. In many ways, boundaries have been portrayed as necessary to healthy relationships while also being overused and ambiguously described.

Henry Cloud defines a boundary as "a personal property line that marks those things for which we are responsible. In other words, boundaries define who we are and who we are not."[1]

Terri Cole defines boundaries as "your own personal rules of engagement—your preferences, limits and deal-breakers."[2]

I define a boundary as a line or limit that is created to protect something that matters.

While the definition may vary, the intention behind a boundary does not. The point of a boundary is to protect something you care about. That could be your time, energy, emotions, physical body, or something else. While boundaries are important, for many people it's difficult to create and communicate a boundary.

Some of the reasons for this are:

1. You might lose the relationship.
2. You don't know what to say.
3. You have trained the other person to believe that you don't have boundaries.
4. The boundary might lead to an uncomfortable conversation or conflict.

Think of a tool that could be incredibly useful to someone, but they don't use it and even avoid it because they don't know how it works. The most important part of having a boundary is making it known that you have one.

If people don't know that you have boundaries, they are likely to blow past them because they simply did not know. To have a boundary conversation, find a time and place that are conducive to talking, and tell the other person what your boundary is.

Here are some examples of boundaries:

1. I won't work more than forty-five hours per week.
2. I won't have more than two drinks.
3. If yelling starts, I will be taking a break from the conversation.

Share your boundary. For close relationships, it may be good to give a brief explanation of the boundary. For a work relationship or relationship in which you are not trying to develop depth, further explanation is often not helpful. The next step is vital and is one that many people miss: You want to encourage the person to respect the boundary.

In one of the examples from above, this might sound like: "Hi Dan, I wanted to communicate a boundary that I have about my work schedule. I won't be working more than forty-five hours per week. This boundary is rooted in my desire for work/life balance. I'd like to talk about how we can make sure that I get done what I need to in that amount of time."

The last sentence is key. The reason is this: Many people approach boundaries as though they are a punishment or threat, creating a situation in which people respond in kind. In psychology, this is called *symmetrical escalation*: People tend to respond with similar tone and emotion to that of the person communicating with them. So, when you communicate a boundary as if it's a punishment, people tend to see it as one rather than as an opportunity to honor what someone else finds important.

Sidenote: If someone shares a boundary with you and invites you to continue your relationship, this is fantastic news because you now know what matters to that person—and you know that *you* matter to that person.

If you are looking to connect well with someone, start by identifying what they want to protect and why. When you know why someone has a boundary, you also know what they value. If you are a Harbor or Peacemaker and need inspiration, look to Advocates and Thinkers as role models. Advocates naturally identify and communicate boundaries while Thinkers tend to identify boundaries that appeal to facts and logic.

When You've Been Hurt

Getting hurt is the worst.

Sometimes people hurt you intentionally, and other times hurt comes from a mishap or misunderstanding. Regardless of the cause, there tend to be a few distinct reactions to being hurt:

1. Withdraw
2. Fight
3. Pretend you aren't hurt

If you are like me, it's immediately obvious when your feelings get hurt, and there is not much you can do to pretend otherwise (although I try). I've always been a bit embarrassed by this—I'd rather be stoic and a bit more mysterious—but alas, I am a bad actor and so if I'm hurt, you can probably guess as much from my body language and eyes. For other people, withdrawing or fighting is their typical reaction. There's no one right approach, only varying costs and consequences for each.

In most cases, the best response when heightened emotions arise is to take a measured and regulated approach. You might need to take some time to breathe, go for a walk, journal what you are feeling, or engage in some other activity that helps you to regulate your emotions.

When your emotions are regulated and you are ready to talk, use the BRIDGE structure to share what hurt you. The conversation should be succinct, and your words should focus on what is true for you while acknowledging that the other person's experience might be different. Although tempting, it is best not to tell the other person what you think their intentions were or demonstrate any other mind-reading capabilities (even if you are genuinely good at gauging others' feelings or motives).

As a sidenote, if you want to tell someone you were hurt but you also don't trust anything they say, stop asking them for a response. I've observed this difficult pattern in couples when one person has broken trust and the other confronts them about a hurtful behavior. After the wounded party shares their hurt, the other person responds, but the responder is quickly met with "I don't believe anything you say." If you have ever experienced or witnessed this type of communication, you know it's painful. The person communicating their hurt is often trying to communicate with a different version of the person sitting in front of them—in their mind, they're talking to a person that they trust. When they realize the person speaking back to them is a version they don't trust, they discount or discredit any kind of response.

Rather than doing this, simply share what you need to and put a period on your final sentence. Not everything needs a response or explanation. If you are unlikely to believe anything someone might say, it is not necessary to invite them to explain. If you wish to give them a brief period to explain but still do not believe anything they say, it is best to respond with "I have heard your explanation, and I will take this into consideration" or even simply "Thank you for your effort to explain."

What you don't want to do is advertise that you're looking for a relational conversation when that is not, in fact, what you want.

When You've Hurt Someone

Dang! What happened?

Hurting others is a given in any long-term relationship, but owning responsibility for the hurts we cause is much less of a certainty. While this may seem unfortunate, there is a beautiful upside: Your ability to respond to and care for the person you hurt is one of the greatest opportunities to demonstrate care and develop relational depth.

In my experience, people struggle with taking responsibility for hurting someone else because they fall into one of two unhealthy categories:

1. They take responsibility for everything.
2. They take responsibility for nothing.

Extremes are rarely a good thing, and these are no different. When you take responsibility for everything, everything seems to be your fault. And while this might seem to be a good approach for someone who is conflict avoidant, over time it creates a precedent that tells the other person what Taylor Swift sang about when she said, "I'm the problem, it's me." While this makes for great pop music, it's terrible for relationships, because who do you think of when there's a problem and no one takes responsibility? That's right—the person who frequently advertises that they are always at fault.

On the other hand, it's equally bad to *never* take responsibility. This approach is perhaps more obviously negative, so I'll explain where I think it comes from. The people I've known and worked with who were the least likely to take responsibility were nearly always the people who believed that a mistake, misstep, or failure said something about their worth. When we view mistakes as implying something about our character and worth, our knee-jerk reaction is often to defend our sense of self by denying we made a mistake.

So, let's say you and another person have hurt each other; you are seemingly balanced in your responsibility taking and now need to have a conversation. This is the first question to consider: Do you know what hurt the other person—in their own words? If you don't, it's important to find out. Apologies that don't land are ones that don't address the actual hurt.

The next step is to ask the other person to have a conversation at a time and place that suits them. During that conversation, own your part as succinctly as possible and share what you would have liked to have done instead.

Do not explain why you did what you did unless you are asked to. Not everyone wants or needs an explanation, and explanations frequently cause further arguments anyway. If asked to explain, you can, and if not asked, you can offer—but resist the urge to reactively explain your thought process.

Here's a great example of what to say in a conversation like this:

> When I said ______ I recognize that it was hurtful to you because _________. I sincerely apologize for saying this and, upon reflection, I wish that I had said/done _________. Would you like me to explain my thought process or expand on why I did what I did?

Here are a few additional notes about taking responsibility:

1. Be specific. People feel seen when you use specific examples.
2. Be genuine or don't do it. The only thing worse than getting hurt is getting a half-hearted apology.
3. If you were also wronged, don't point this out during your apology. Own your part first, and then once your part has been addressed, you can ask the person to discuss how you were hurt.
4. If the person is not satisfied with your apology, ask why and consider refining what you said.
5. Allow the person to still feel hurt afterward.

When You Have a Need

First, I'd like to congratulate you for having a need. Seriously. I work with many clients who have unfortunately never identified a need or been asked what they need, and so the very idea that they have a need and should communicate it is a big deal.

Defined in terms of a relationship, a need is something that is of vital importance to your continuing in the relationship. Because it is of vital importance, it is necessary to communicate it.

An easy way to communicate a need is to state it simply and then describe how it might be met. The "how it might be met" part is important, because, if the other person doesn't share your need, they may struggle to meet it without having some direction on how to do so.

You might communicate a need in the following way: "I wanted to share with you that one of my needs is to have time to complete my devotional each day. The devotional takes about fifteen minutes. I prefer to do it in the morning, but it could also be done at night if need be. Can you accommodate this?"

If your need is dismissed, questioned, or challenged, refrain from justifying it and instead explain it further using different words. The reason I say this is because if you have, in fact, identified your need as a need, getting the other person to understand or agree with the need is of low importance. For instance, if my need is to wear copious amounts of sunscreen to prevent skin cancer anytime I am exposed to the sun (thanks, pasty white skin and Dutch heritage!), there is little need for back-and-forth about whether the need is legitimate or makes sense to others. To some it will, and to others it won't. The important thing is that others are willing to honor that it's my need.

Here are a few notes about needs:

1. You shouldn't have twenty-seven needs. Remember that a need is something vital.
2. You are allowed and encouraged to have needs. When you tell someone your need, you are effectively telling them how they can show you love.
3. When you communicate your need, use a posture of "I'm telling you what's true for me" rather than "I have a need if it's okay with you?"
4. If you aren't sure what you need and are testing something out, just say so and reserve the right to change your mind.
5. Some communication types will have a more difficult time than others with needs. Peacemakers, Harbors, and Thinkers sometimes struggle with identifying and communicating needs.

When You Have an Opinion

The decision of whether to share an opinion comes down almost exclusively to the audience and the ask. In many situations, an opinion is not asked for, needed, or wanted and instead is simply tolerated. However, we can share opinions in meaningful ways to an audience that is receptive.

Here are some examples of times when an opinion is likely not helpful:

1. When someone is sharing something vulnerable or a problem they are experiencing.
2. When the opinion is inflammatory or may shut down the conversation.
3. When the opinion serves only you and not the conversation.

And here are some examples of times when an opinion may be helpful:

1. When it is asked for.
2. When it is necessary, such as in matters of safety, concern, and well-being.
3. When you are in a setting that encourages the sharing of opinions.

Remember that hard conversations don't have to be painful. In fact, they are opportunities in disguise. They tell people we care and invite them to meet us in that same spirit. Without hard conversations, you never really know where you stand and if you are overinvested or underinvested in a relationship. So, while you might not look forward to having them, your willingness to engage in hard conversations signals that you value your relationships. Make sure to find others who value relationships like you do, and then practice what you've learned in this chapter.

Reflect

1. Which of the topics in this chapter resonated with you?
2. What lesson in this chapter do you wish you would have learned earlier in your life?
3. Do you struggle to identify your needs? Spend some time considering what your needs include and discuss them with a trusted friend.
4. Are you quick to share your opinion, or are you more reserved? Should you change your relationship with your opinions?
5. Who do you wish would read this chapter and why?

CHAPTER 13

Practicing Communication

By now you have read most of this book, know your communication type, and are full of insight and awareness.

This is an excellent start—but it's only the start.

In his 1926 book *The Story of Philosophy*, Will Durant describes the philosophy of Aristotle this way: "We are what we repeatedly do. Excellence, then, is not an act, but a habit."

Establishing habits of good communication is where most people get off track. While I would like to believe that I have taught you the best possible tools for communicating well in any relationship, being good at healthy communication means practicing other PATHS styles frequently. When we become fluent in PATHS other than our own, relationships and connection thrive.

People are occasionally disappointed when they discover that not only do they need to learn about communication, but they also need to practice it more than once. It's like the time I bought a fancy exercise bike without realizing that to get in shape I also needed to use it. As tempting as it was, I couldn't just sit on the bike and watch Netflix. I had to first learn to use the bike and then actually use it.

I am reminded of a time when I was speaking at a conference and got to meet someone I respect a great deal. Jon Acuff is a fellow author and speaker and is a genuine guy, and it was an amazing experience to speak with him. After I gave my keynote, I met up with him in the green room, and he excitedly told me that he thought I'd done a great job. He then proceeded to go over a bunch of notes he had taken about what worked, what could be refined, and what he thought stood out. I was thrilled to get these notes from Jon, but our conversation highlighted a point relevant to the idea of practicing communication.

If you want to be good at something, reading about it isn't enough. Whether you are a seasoned speaker or someone who struggles with small talk, practice is necessary. This is true no matter what type of communicator you want to be, and whether you're a speaker, teacher, leader, parent, or spouse.

Practice is necessary, but *focused* practice is what actually moves the needle. That means practicing speaking to your intended audience using their PATHS style, rather than just using the style you are most fluent in.

The greatest communication problem for most people is apathy. And apathy eventually leads to atrophy, because communicating well doesn't happen in isolation. It requires community and genuine interaction, which means being in places where people are talking and connecting.

Here are some reasons to practice:

1. We are stronger and healthier when we are known.
2. Sometimes people need to talk to us.
3. Relationships cannot be forged or maintained without communication.
4. Wisdom literature, including the Bible (see Proverbs 27:17), talks about the importance of communicating with others.

Related to the second item on the list above—the one about people needing to talk to us—consider the following statistics:

- 59 percent of employees do not ask for help at work.[1]
- 58 percent of individuals with mental illness avoid seeking support.[2]
- 58 percent of students report feeling reluctant to ask for help with mental health concerns.[3]

As someone who has spoken to many struggling people, I will tell you that practicing communication is not just good for you but can also be lifesaving for someone else. I cannot tell you how many times I have spoken to someone with genuine interest only to find that they were struggling significantly.

Sometimes people need to be asked.

People rarely regret reaching out to someone to see if they need to talk. Instead, what fills us with regret is not reaching out and learning later that the person had been praying for someone to ask them a question. It's not your job to talk to everyone, but imagine how different the world would be if we simply talked to the people we already know. I want to live in that world, because in that world people struggle less and relationships thrive.

Now that you've committed to practicing, let's talk about a few ways to practice and keep the momentum going.

Visualization

Research by Dr. Alan Richardson at the University of Chicago has shown that visualizing is nearly as powerful as practicing. In his study, a third of the players on a basketball team practiced free throws each day, another third visualized taking shots and making them, and the remaining third did nothing at all.[4]

Who do you think improved?

Surprisingly, the first two groups improved at nearly the same level. Brain research tells us that this is because visualizing something and experiencing something activate our brains in similar ways.

This is wonderful to know, because it means we can visualize having a conversation with someone and essentially practice what we want to say before we actually say it.

I have been using this technique for years before important conversations, speaking engagements, and retreats.

To practice, I sit down in a quiet, dark room (usually in the morning) and literally think through each step of what I am about to do and what it would look like to do it well.

Some of the questions I consider include:

1. What would I hope to say?
2. Where could things go awry, and what could I say or do if that happened?
3. How would I like to feel as I am communicating?

4. What can I do to ensure that my audience connects with my words?
5. What PATHS style am I speaking to, and what will resonate with them?
6. How does my own style help or hinder my message?

After visualizing the scenario and considering all the details above, I conclude with a simple prayer asking God to help me be a good steward of the gifts I've been given and honor him with my communication.

That's it.

Visualizing doesn't solve every problem or make actual practice obsolete, but it has helped tremendously with my confidence and anxiety before important conversations, because it feels as though I have had them already.

Writing It Out

Another helpful technique is to write out what you want to say and how you want to say it. Many people struggle with knowing what they want to say without spending time to identify it first. If this is you, rather than try to become wired differently, embrace your need to write things out first. Start by jotting down the basics like what you want to say, what feeling you want to communicate, and what outcome you want from the conversation. This practice will help you feel more prepared and gain clarity.

If you are anxious about the conversation, it's also helpful to write out what you are anxious about and what, if anything, could help you feel differently.

Bestselling author and entrepreneur Tim Ferriss uses a technique he calls "fear-setting," in which he asks himself, "What if I defined my fears instead of my goals?"

In this exercise, Tim recommends defining the worst thing that could happen if you took the action you're wanting to avoid, followed by how you could prevent that worst-case scenario and also what you could do to repair the situation if the worst-case scenario happened.

Naming and then thinking through ways to combat your fears is an excellent way to reduce fear and anxiety and boost your confidence about moving forward.

Practice When the Stakes Are Low

One of my favorite places to practice communication skills is at the airport. I think this is mostly because it's a place where most people abandon communication skills. It's not unusual to hear someone talking loudly, heatedly, or even confusingly (I tried asking for directions at a not-to-be-named airport and left very, very confused). The point is this: Most of the people you see at an airport or on an airplane aren't people you are going to see again. For that reason, practicing communication skills there is a pretty safe bet.

Before I leave for the airport on a travel day, I often challenge myself to talk to three people during that day's travel. Any degree of conversation counts; my only agenda is to keep the conversation going until it naturally stops. This practice has led to several friendships and some unbelievable stories of meeting people I never would have met otherwise.

Once I spoke with a certain Atlanta-based rapper at the airport, and we shared our mutual love of collecting sneakers. Prior to this conversation, I had no idea who this person was, but I took a chance because I saw that we both were wearing the same sneaker brand and style. This led to further conversation and a commitment to staying in touch.

Not every interaction will have this outcome, but it doesn't matter. The point is to get good at connecting and to make someone's day better because of your effort. When you can do this, everyone wins.

Another way to practice when the stakes are low is to schedule a weekly check-in with a friend where you can tell them the whole truth. You know, the whole truth. Not the truth you might post on Instagram or tell a colleague, but the actual reality of how you are doing. Commit to letting the other person share honestly and vulnerably too.

This is a fantastic exercise for two reasons. The first is that you develop a deeper relationship with your friend because you are diving deep. The second is that when you practice being honest and authentic on a regular basis, it becomes much easier to do it when it counts.

The best version of this exercise is to do it with the person or people who matter most to you. If you can get in the habit of going deep regularly, you will be able to conquer most difficult conversations that come your way. Much of our difficulty in connecting with the people we love is related to our lack of ongoing vulnerability and communication.

You might consider doing a weekly check-in where you:

1. Discuss a high point for the week.
2. Discuss a low point for the week.
3. Ask for something you need. If you can't think of

anything you need, ask for something you want. Many times, people want to show up for us but don't know how. Make it easy for them.

4. Express gratitude for something the other person did in the last week. Be specific. Rather than saying "You were nice on Tuesday," say "When you asked about my day on Tuesday, it meant a lot to me."
5. Tell them the thing that you need to tell them but don't want to. You know, the problem you are struggling with or even just an emotion you've been feeling lately. Let them in if they are safe, and watch your relationship grow.

Be Around People Who Do It Better Than You

I will never forget walking into a mastermind group in Nashville where I was surrounded by fifty leaders, founders, speakers, and more. The room buzzed with energy, and everywhere I looked, beautiful people were smiling and having conversations. I sat nervously at an out-of-the-way table and was quickly joined by someone who did not seem the least bit nervous. We struck up a conversation, and when they left to talk to someone else, I felt empowered. The room was filled with pro communicators, both literally and figuratively. These people could speak from a stage and share hurts and heartaches. I learned a lot from the people in that room.

One of them was a speaker, Dan Martell, who shared some of his story as well as the idea of "going pro" in business, which is adapted from Steven Pressfield's work. From Dan's perspective, when we find something that matters in life, we have a decision to make. Dan said that in his life, he had decided to "go pro" with his business and brand. For him, this meant practicing and committing to learning consistently so he could be better. The idea was inspiring because at the end of the day we get to decide how we show up in our life, business, and relationships.

When it comes to your communication, do you want to go pro? If you do, you will need to practice.

Here's what's at stake if you don't:

1. Your relationships will lack impact and depth.
2. You will struggle to be truly seen, heard, and understood.
3. The people close to you won't know where they stand.
4. Your career and success will not be as robust as they could be.
5. You will struggle to work through difficult conversations.

The beauty of practicing is that you will only be better for it. The best things in my life today wouldn't be present if I didn't know how to communicate well and build relationships. All these things have come from my ability to ask questions, connect, and share with others.

It feels a little bold to say this, but there is probably no better skill to invest your time and energy into learning than communicating well, both about your PATHS type and other PATHS types. The facets of our life that matter most are closely related to our ability to communicate.

The best way to practice communication consistently is to

build a life that requires you to communicate often. Some of us tend to isolate, but it is only by stepping into our discomfort and being willing to have conversations that we will change ourselves—and change the world.

You Might Get Hit by the Ball

One of the greatest risks of building a relationship that matters is that things will get broken. Feelings will be hurt; we will be injured. Sometimes even practice leads to heartache.

If you've been hurt before, it can feel daunting to try again, because who wants to continue to get hurt? I have played racquetball quite a bit in my life, and I once played with a friend who had never played before. I was doing my best to go easy on him, but at one point the ball hit him in the back of the head. I didn't mean to do it, was terribly sorry, and apologized at least twenty-five times. But my friend looked at me and said, "I think I'm good with stopping here."

I pressed him a little, because I was thrilled to have a new racquetball partner, but my friend continued: "This is not something I need to do. It's not something I want to do. It hurt, and now my racquetball career is over."

And just like that, it was over. Now, how many times do we do that same thing when relationships hurt us? We get beamed by the ball, we get hit by the racket, we twist our ankle, we don't have fun, it doesn't end well. And then we end up saying, "Why would I want to do that again?"

Sometimes practicing means experiencing betrayal, which for many is among the worst pains they've experienced. If you trust your partner, spouse, or colleague and have been betrayed, you know that it can break your heart. If you have survived a broken heart, you understand the hesitation to try again.

And yet, strangely we usually want to try again, because we're drawn to relationships even though they can cause hurt. While we all realize that being in a relationship carries a risk of getting hurt, some of us acknowledge that we can hurt others too. Practice makes perfect but is not perfect in itself.

You are worth practicing for, and whoever you choose for a romantic or personal relationship should be willing to practice too. I see too many relationships in which one person is out scoring goals on the soccer field of communication every night while the other person is watching TV at home. Choose people who will practice with you and for you. When you do, it changes everything.

Reflect

1. Where is your favorite place to practice communication, or who is your favorite person to practice with?
2. What is one small step you can take this week to practice communication?
3. Is there someone who has been on your mind recently who you need to reach out to? Can you do it today?

CHAPTER 14

Responding to Hard Things

Now that we have mastered saying hard things ourselves, it's time to address what to do when someone says something challenging to us. Many of my clients (and many people in general) are good at either saying or receiving hard things, but few are good at both. However, how you respond to difficult words is just as important as how you communicate them.

Consider your communication path and attachment style. Both factor into your communication in the sense that they speak to the *why* behind what you say. So when someone is saying something challenging or vulnerable to you, it's important to consider *why* they are saying these things. When you understand communication paths, this becomes easier and allows you to get right to the point.

In addition to considering the other person's communication path, there are several other helpful factors to keep in mind as you listen to their words.

Posture

Have you ever thought about what you're communicating through your posture when someone is talking with you? Posture matters because it tells the other person how you are experiencing what they're telling you. If 93 percent of communication is nonverbal, that means that if someone is sharing something with you and you are lying down, slouching, hunched over, or aggressively leaning forward, they will have a difficult time trusting that you are engaged.[1] What's more, in couples sessions, I will sometimes see heavily tattooed and tough-looking adult men slink down in their chairs as their wife shares about her feelings. Unfortunately, these men often resemble children being reprimanded by their mother, and that is not the type of relationship most women want.

I came face-to-face with the importance of posture while getting certified for a specialty as a therapist. I was tasked to send in a video of myself doing therapy (the client consented and was not onscreen). Because of the way the video needed to be shot, I could see only myself listening and interacting but was able to hear both myself and my client talking.

Let's just say it was an eye-opening experience from the start. Although I had imagined it would be kind of like when college football players review tapes of games, it was not like that at all. As I watched the tape, I noticed immediately that I appeared much less famed psychologist Carl Rogers (like I had hoped) and much more pro wrestler bouncing on the corner post of a wrestling ring waiting to be tagged in. It was truly cringeworthy, and so after watching enough of the tape to be embarrassed, I committed to trying again.

The second time, my voice was barely audible, and I sat in my chair like Jell-O poured into a mold. I did not resemble anyone you would want to tell something important to and, quite frankly, looked as though I had several of my own problems to sort through.

The third video was finally better, probably because I was becoming familiar with what not to do.

When it's your turn to listen, do it better than I did. Instead of slinking or slouching, sit up straight. If you are in a place where good posture is difficult to maintain, ask to sit somewhere else. Be willing to sit up and tune in.

Your Face

If you look annoyed when someone is talking to you, they are likely to think, well, that you are annoyed. Not everyone has a resting face that looks inviting, and not paying attention to how you look can create real disconnect during an important conversation. Many times, people who don't look friendly actually are but just don't look it. If this is you, a little awareness can go a long way. If you are prone to having a resting cranky face (RCF), it's helpful to ask the other person how you appear to be receiving what they are saying. This gives you an opportunity to reassure them if they think you are angry and you aren't. This alone stops lots of arguments, because it is difficult to imagine that someone is carefully listening to you if they appear to be grimacing or wincing. We may incorrectly assume that the other person is angry, annoyed, or worse.

The Environment

For people who are sensitive to distractions, it's especially important to be aware of how the environment is impacting them. For instance, if you are wanting to have an important conversation with someone who struggles to stay present and focused, having that conversation at a busy coffee shop may not be the best idea. If the environment cannot be helped and you are trying to focus but find yourself distracted, it's helpful to say so. Think of the environment as the table setting for your conversation. You want to set the table for the type of conversation you are about to have. Some conversations are private-booth-at-a-steakhouse type conversations, while others could be done at McDonald's. Have you ever had a conversation in a place that didn't fit?

When receiving someone else's vulnerable or important story, it's important to be aware that they may assume you'll have the worst reaction possible to what they are sharing, especially if they have had any sort of attachment wounding (think anxious, avoidant, or disorganized). While this is not entirely your problem, it is something you can help them with. And helping them is easier to do if you begin to see what they are saying as a gift. Any insight into someone's inner world is a gift and should be heard (even if you disagree). Vulnerability is the key to deeper relationships, so please don't look past someone's effort to share what's on their heart.

Do you remember the story of the woman who washed Jesus's feet with expensive perfume and wiped them with her hair? The disciples disagreed with her choices, but Jesus understood that for her, these actions were as vulnerable and loving as it gets. Rather than scolding her, he embraced that, for her, this was a big deal. This is the type of energy we want to bring into our relationships. For the other person, this is a big deal, and that's enough.

Other Helpful Things to Consider

If you want to get even closer in your relationships, practice saying, "If it matters to you, it matters to me."

This statement has been a game changer in many of the relationships I have helped to repair and improve. On a deep level, we all want to know that what we think, feel, and say matters. And when we hear this affirmed by the people who matter most to us, it helps us feel understood in a way we might not have felt before.

When you use a statement like this, recognize the power it has but also the responsibility it puts on you. If you tell someone that their concerns matter to you, you need to act in a way that communicates that you mean it. A common problem in relationships occurs when someone communicates with depth and intimacy, but their actions don't align with their words, which often leads the other person to invoke the old cliché "talk is cheap." While I understand the sentiment, I think a better version is this:

> Talk and action are the original dynamic duo of communication in healthy relationships.

Both are needed in any relationship, and a relationship suffers if one of them is missing. It's common to struggle with one more than the other, so it's worth thinking about whether you're better at talking or doing.

If you are good at doing, then you're in great hands with everything you have learned in this book. Now, as Nike says, "Just do it."

But if you struggle in the doing department, here's what you need to know.

You must detach yourself from the idea that your worth is attached to what you promise to do. The clients who I see struggling most with overpromising and underdelivering are often men who do not feel confident or adequate. In an attempt to be better, they learn to repeat what other men are doing that seemingly works. While this is a nice thought, in the world of relationships, trouble is sure to follow when we simply parrot what others say in their relationships.

What you say will always carry more weight when it's authentic to you. In personal relationships, people prefer authenticity and vulnerability over style and elegance. And action wins consistently over aspiration. If someone makes themselves vulnerable by sharing something risky or saying something uncomfortable, they want to know that you are willing to risk the same thing. Vulnerability without discernment isn't connecting; it's compromising.

Early in the promotion of my first book, *Get Past Your Past*, I did several podcast interviews. I was often asked the same first question: "Tell me about your life. Help us to get to know you."

If you've heard the later interviews, you probably heard a succinct answer to this question that clocked in at a minute or less and kept my dignity intact. However, that was not always the case.

Imagine having written your first book and feeling all the excitement that comes with it. You show up to your first podcast recording bright-eyed and bushy-tailed, sweating profusely and incredibly nervous that you will say the wrong thing. Because you wanted to be clearheaded for the interview, you ran several miles before getting ready, and now you're on camera, purple-faced and ready to go.

And then you get asked a question that is completely open for interpretation.

Being an analytical guy, I decided a chronological answer would be best, so I went ahead and started with the hospital where I was born.

I think I was talking about my awkward elementary school years and odd fascination with the bubonic plague when I started to notice the interviewer seeming a bit distracted.

When I shared my deep feelings about wearing headgear with my braces as a seventh grader it became more obvious that I had severely overshot the question.

In an act that can only be described as pure genius, about fifteen minutes into my monologue I finally realized I was oversharing and then said (immediately after the terrible braces story), "And I guess that brings us to today."

The interviewer looked stunned, my team was flabbergasted, and I felt incredibly stupid.

I think we've all experienced some version of this. You know, that feeling when we put ourselves out there and regret it. That feeling is what happens when someone tells you something vulnerable and you respond with defensiveness, guardedness, or withdrawal. No matter how much people say they don't care what others say or think, no one wants to be the only one that is vulnerable. It's too risky and hurts too much if we fail.

Here are a few ways you can respond well when someone tells you something important:

Relate to their thought process or emotion. You might not feel the way they do or think the way they think, but try to relate to some part of what was shared.

Keep the conversation going. Understand that the moment you shift into problem-solving, make the conversation about you, or pull out your phone, the moment is over. Be present.

Ask a question. Try starting with one of these: "Can you tell me more about that?" "What's that been like for you?" "Have you ever experienced this before?"

Identify why they are telling you and offer help accordingly. If they're just looking for understanding, do your best not to offer resources, and if they are venting, know that it's not your job to solve their problems.

When people let you in and tell you something vulnerable, they don't usually continue to do it if it goes poorly.

A couple years ago I was on a whale-watching cruise during a couples retreat I hosted in Cabo San Lucas. During this cruise, it seemed like dolphins were everywhere, jumping out of the water and putting on a big show. The whales were different. Their trips to the surface were quick and infrequent. I asked one of the crew members about this, and they said that dolphins come up to the surface much more often than whales do because whales tend to live in the depths. This has stuck with me ever since I heard it, because I think that in relationships, some people are like those whales—when they come to the surface, it's a big deal. And just like in whale watching, if you miss their appearance, it will be a long time before it happens again. So, when someone tells you how they feel or gets vulnerable with you, treat it with the importance it deserves.

Remember that, for some people, surfacing to tell you how they feel may take all the courage they have. If you fail to meet them when they surface, they may decide not to try again—or at the very least they'll be much less likely to try in the future.

Here are a few tips to help you listen and respond well:

1. Sit up straight in your chair.
2. Speak with your normal volume and tone (even if someone is upset with you).
3. Look at the person speaking. This is important, and while it may be tough if you are neurodivergent, it's worth trying to do.
4. Verify your understanding of what has been said by recapping it back to the speaker. If you get lost, say so and ask a question.
5. Be patient and don't rush the other person.

Remember that when someone cares enough to tell you how they are thinking and feeling, they are worthy of your full attention. You would hope for the same.

Also know that every PATHS style has certain listening behaviors that they naturally do well. For example, Sparks are naturally expressive and charismatic. Harbors are great at making space for others, and Advocates are amazing encouragers. As you consider how to better connect with those who share their feelings with you, resist the urge to focus only on where you struggle and instead acknowledge where you succeed too.

Reflect

1. What is your biggest challenge when someone is sharing something important with you?

2. What is one small step you could take today to improve in this area?
3. Is there a difficult or challenging conversation you have been avoiding?
4. What might it look like to lean into your discomfort and have the conversation?
5. What could help you show up authentically and vulnerably when having a meaningful conversation?

CHAPTER 15

Communicating with the Uncommunicative

Not everyone deserves a front-
row seat in your life.
—ANNE LAMOTT

Early in my career as a therapist I met a couple who'd had an on-again, off-again relationship for several years. While the man wanted to get married and have children, his partner was ambivalent, and the longer the relationship went on, the higher the pressure mounted. The couple would have periods of time when the relationship was seemingly wonderful; they got along, felt connected, and talked about the future. But these times would never last, and eventually the relationship would descend into yelling, insults, and accusations.

Our interactions in therapy began during one of the couple's good times; we were able to laugh and joke with one another, and a therapeutic relationship was formed. Along the way, I challenged both parties to develop emotional maturity and communication skills. All seemed to be working well until one day when the couple came in and admitted they were having a difficult time. They were not kidding. What unfolded in front of me that day was the vitriol they had alluded to for weeks. I attempted to intervene at several points, and eventually one of them began insulting me the way they had been insulting their partner.

That was when I decided that we needed to pause the conversation until such time that boundaries and decency could be honored. I ensured that the couple was okay to leave, and they left my office. Shortly afterward, I received a message apologizing for what had happened, along with a promise that it would never happen again.

When the couple returned the following week, I'll admit that I was hesitant about the session, but things went calmly. I hoped that the previous week had simply been an off week between the couple, but I quickly learned that wasn't the case. The next session was immediately explosive and ended the same way the other one had, with the only difference being that I didn't wait as long to call it.

I eventually needed to refer the couple to another therapist who I hoped might be able to help, and when I did, I had a profound realization about communication:

> Healthy communication is invite-only, and not everyone is willing or able to show up.

People pleasers, Peacemakers, and people with insecure attachment, listen up: No amount of education or communication know-how will change someone who does not want to communicate (or learn to communicate) in a healthy manner. More succinctly, you being good at communication does not make up for the other person actively choosing to be bad at it. It doesn't matter if you are fluent in a language if the other person refuses to speak to you.

Trying to communicate with someone who won't put in any effort is like dancing the foxtrot with a partner who refuses to learn the steps. You could be the best dancer in the world, but you will not be able to overcome their unwillingness to learn the dance. This was disheartening for me to realize as a therapist. After all the time I had put into my education, I had figured that if anyone could coax people into communicating, I could. And while this was a nice thought, it was probably more related to a childhood where winning people over was the norm than it was a viable plan for the present.

When we're faced with someone who doesn't seem to be participating in the communication dance, it's imperative that we discern which of the following categories applies: can't dance but is willing, or won't dance and refuses to learn? Of these two potential partners, only one is possible to work with: those who can't dance but are willing to learn. Sure, our toes might get stepped on occasionally, and they may lose the beat, but the willingness is what counts.

So, what do you do when someone is willing to learn but the initial attempts at communication haven't been healthy?

You first must answer a few questions for yourself and for the other person.

1. Is This Safe?

The word *safety* has been overused in the mental health community lately, and unfortunately that has led to some discounting of the premise behind it as well as questions about what it really means to be safe. Many people struggle to understand safety in the context of emotional intimacy and to discern the difference between safety and comfort—so a better definition must be identified. To be safe in a given conversation is to believe that the other person will not intentionally hurt you, and to agree on appropriate boundaries and ground rules for the conversation.

The first part of this definition is obvious in the sense that if you are entering into communication with someone you know will intentionally hurt you, it is not safe. The second part, establishing ground rules, is a little trickier.

It is important to identify what safety means to you. Some ideas for boundaries might be the following:

1. I am physically safe.
2. I believe the person I'm communicating with values my safety.
3. We agree about what escalation looks like and what to do if it happens.
4. I believe the person I'm communicating with has neutral or positive intentions.
5. I am willing to abide by my own definition of safety.

If you are not sure about any of the above, ask some questions to better determine how to proceed. And it's worth restating that you must be willing to abide by your own definition of safety in your behavior. Setting expectations for safety that you are unwilling or unable to follow is just as unhealthy as not setting them at all.

2. Is It Necessary?

Similar to safety, necessity falls on a spectrum. How do we really know when a conversation is necessary? Consider some of Jesus's interactions with the Pharisees when they were trying to hurt him and were asking him trick questions. While these conversations were far from healthy, it was in fact necessary for Jesus to engage in them from the standpoint that he needed to speak truth into situations where the truth was not being spoken. For this reason, he talked to people who were mostly unwilling to listen. However, the rest of his audience heard every word, and for them it was life-giving.

Necessity is subjective, but the truth isn't.

As I have become a more seasoned therapist, I've noticed that many conversations I felt were necessary when I was younger seem much less necessary today. I think the reason for this is that the longer you communicate with people, the easier it becomes to identify the degree to which a conversation is likely to be helpful. For me, the main filter I use to determine if a conversation is necessary is whether it is likely to be helpful to either party. If the answer is no, then the conversation is most likely not necessary.

How do you define necessity when considering whether you should talk with someone?

3. Am I Willing to Tell the Truth and Receive Their Truth?

This question might surprise you a bit. It may seem obvious that we should tell the truth, but telling the truth also means we should avoid placating, people-pleasing, and telling half-truths. This is especially important for conversations in which conflict is likely or expected, because in these difficult moments, sometimes we aren't so good at saying what needs to be said.

Some of the greatest change I've seen in clients has come after a session in which I told them the truth. This is not to say that I typically lie to my clients; rather, stating something that is uncomfortable but true often produces profound results. This happened when I met with a leader who had flown to see me; after talking nonstop for over ninety minutes, he shared with me that he had always considered himself a wonderful listener and conversationalist. In that moment, I had a decision to make: Should I placate my client and hope for the best, or tell him the truth about my experience of him so far? I kindly and compassionately explained that the truth about my time with him was that I hadn't experienced him that way at all. My client was shocked; he immediately texted his assistant and asked for complete honesty regarding this topic. When my client's phone dinged a few seconds later, I saw him shake his head in dismay. "How could I not have known, and why didn't anyone tell me?" We must be willing to tell the truth even if it's uncomfortable.

Perhaps the only part harder than telling the truth is being willing to receive it and take it into consideration. Note that I did not say to internalize it or agree blindly, but it's important to at least consider what someone tells us about what's true for them. In the previous story, my client could have considered what I said and discarded it, thus keeping the problem and avoiding the truth. We have all been guilty of this. But the question remains: Are you willing to receive another person's truth, even if it is something you disagree with or are unsure about?

4. Is This a Relationship That I Want or Need to Pour Into?

Everyone has different criteria for deciding whether to pour into a relationship, but it is still an important question to consider. Is the person you're speaking with someone you want or need to develop a relationship with? In the instance of a romantic relationship, this might be a resounding "Yes!" Other times, you might find yourself considering a friendship or work relationship for which the answer is more difficult to decide.

If you do not want or need to pour into a relationship, your communication should match the degree to which you value the relationship. What I mean by this is that if you do not feel you need or want to go deeper in the relationship, then it's okay to keep your conversations surface level and cordial. Not everyone needs to be your best friend. You can still talk with them, but pouring yourself out may not be required.

Sometimes your answer to the question of whether to pour into a relationship will be "no." For that matter, sometimes other people will decide "no" about you. Deciding whether to invest in a relationship doesn't mean deciding the other person is better or worse, deserving or undeserving, valuable or not; instead, your goal should be to realize what the best communicators know:

Great communication won't make someone listen if they are committed to not hearing you.

The Best Approach

The best approach to identifying whom you should have important conversations with is to trust your gut. And I don't mean that in a New Age crystals sort of way. What I mean is that if you immediately get a bad feeling about someone, listen to that feeling and ask questions.

Also, identify where the other person is at in terms of their desire to connect, and meet them with the energy needed. Notice that I didn't say you should meet someone on their level, because in the case of someone committed to unhealthy or poor communication, that would mean diminishing yourself. Instead, meet the other person with the energy needed to accomplish your goals for the conversation.

For instance, if you know a conversation is unlikely to end well but you still have important information to communicate to the other person, then it's worth having the conversation, but not worth spending your full energy. People get tired and bitter when they consistently give others their full energy in conversations that are clearly unhealthy and unhelpful. So, rather than pouring a great deal of energy into convincing, begging, pleading, or worse, take an emotional step back and detach from the outcome. Commit to speaking the truth, and let the outcome be what it will. Remember that your job as a healthy communicator is not to make others healthier by force, but instead to lead by example. Failure to conserve your energy can lead to a blowup or to saying hurtful things that can't be unsaid.

If you have ever been in a relationship where you frequently tried to talk the other person into practicing healthier communication, you know the cycle. You begin talking, the conversation goes south because they take it there, and you try desperately to hang on. However, eventually you get tired, and your communication becomes harsh and hurtful. The other person is now hurt, and you feel guilty because you know better. You then apologize and take full responsibility for everything until the next conflict occurs.

Instead of repeating this cycle, remember this maxim:

The goal is not knowing better, it's doing better.

Sometimes doing better means stopping before you even get started and understanding that even with the best intentions, trying to talk someone into something they don't want is still trying to talk someone into something they don't want.

Saying No

I have a theory that most romantic relationships are made up of one "yes" person and one "no" person. And, while this can be helpful in some cases—parenting, car purchases, financial management—it can be daunting in others.

This is especially true in times of conflict. It is very difficult to say no when someone else is saying yes. However, if you need to stop a conversation or stopping is in the best interest of the relationship, then saying no is necessary. If you don't, what often happens is the conversation leads to exactly the negative place you thought it would.

To avoid that, if you need to say no, simply say no.

Surprisingly, "No" can be a full sentence.

"Should we keep talking?" No.

"But we need to talk this out right now." No.

"You have to listen to me." No.

These are a few examples of "no" in response to conversations that have gone incredibly awry. In those cases, you can be assured that "no" is enough. In fact, the unhealthier the relationship, the less likely it is that further explanation will improve the situation. There are several reasons for this, but a primary one is that explanations often breed arguments. If someone is already upset about something you said and then you explain your thought process, the explanation is likely to only upset them more (unless they are sincerely asking for it).

Have you ever used GPS and found that it took you to the wrong place? This has happened to me a few times, and it mostly seems to happen before my biggest speaking engagements. One of these times, I ended up driving well out of my way and arrived nearly thirty-five minutes later than I was supposed to. I could tell the host was already upset, but then I thought I should probably explain all the roads I took to get to the wrong place. I was not very far into my explanation when the host said that even if I'd been trying to go to the other place, I could have taken a better road.

One of the most preventable conflicts I see with couples occurs when one of them explains how they got to a conclusion or outcome that the other person doesn't like, without being asked. If you are not asked, recognize that an explanation is likely to upset the person you are talking to. However, if they do ask, tell them! It's not a secret or something you are trying to hide, but it's something not every discussion will call for.

When you tell someone no and want to explain yourself, whether because they are asking or because the relationship is one you value highly, it's still important to be succinct. Explain your basic thought process regarding your decision and leave it there. Resist the urge to argue about whether you should or shouldn't have thought the way you did. The decision already happened, and you are not looking for them to help you rewrite it.

The decision to say no to a conversation is often a very mature decision but is not usually seen as such. This has a lot to do with the packaging around the "no." It's best to state it simply, and if there is hope for further communication, you can share the timeframe at which you plan to return to the conversation. That might be in an hour, day, or week. Be specific, succinct, and steadfast. Do not say no and then get pulled back into the conversation. Let your no be no.

As a sidenote, I have seen many people-pleasing clients say "I can't" instead of saying "No" or "I won't." Although saying "I can't" is a start, it's usually not accurate unless it's actually true that you can't.

Saying "I can't" implies that you could if you were better, tougher, or stronger—but this is not usually why you are saying no. You are saying no because you won't engage further. How you speak about yourself matters, so if you won't have a conversation, just say so. It may be hard for the other person to hear, but it at least lets them know where they stand.

This is ultimately what we all want—to know where we stand and who we stand with, which won't be everyone. Be grateful for the people who stick with you.

Your words matter, and it's important to share them with people who value them. When I talk with someone who feels isolated and exhausted, it's usually because they have been using their words to speak to the wrong audience.

Be careful with your words and intentional with your communication, and honor yourself and others with your voice.

Reflect

1. Is there someone you have stopped communicating with? Why did you stop? What would it take for things to change?
2. Have you ever experienced someone not wanting to talk with you? What did you learn from that experience?
3. What do you consider when thinking about safety in a relationship?
4. What is your tolerance for bad behavior during a conversation? Do you need to rethink your boundaries?
5. Are you quick or slow to deem someone unable to engage in healthy communication with you?

CHAPTER 16

Special Circumstances

In the midst of chaos, there
is also opportunity.
—SUN TZU

In my experience, the times when you most need to communicate well also tend to be the times it's most tempting not to. Messy, challenging, or heated situations test our ability to regulate our emotions, and if we are new to communicating from a healthy place, this can be overwhelming or disconcerting.

I have observed this many times in my career, such as when working with child soldiers, Navy SEALs, severe trauma victims, prison inmates, and people who have built amazing lives that are now falling apart. They all need to work through the messy middle—the parts of their stories that few people talk about because they'd rather simply share the beginning and end of their stories, rather than the parts that didn't go as planned or weren't neat and clean. Stories seem tidier when you share the problem and how you overcame it, rather than the long part in the middle where you didn't know or maybe even lost your way. But you and I both know that most of life takes place in the middle of the field rather than the end zones.

For most of my career, I have specialized in the messy parts. Colleagues, friends, and clients have all asked why I feel drawn to those spaces, and it's tough to explain other than to say that I have been in those places before and know how it feels to be there alone. I also believe that in the messiest and most difficult of times, we can see glimpses of God walking alongside us if we are willing to look.

I tell you all of this because just when you start to feel like you have communication figured out, life is going to get real and you'll likely find yourself wondering what to do next.

That's the reason I wrote this chapter, dedicated to some of the specific messy situations people face—ones they sometimes feel they can't tell anyone about.

To prepare for the messy parts of your own life, you must first take *should* out of your vocabulary. *Should* gets many people in trouble because it implies that what you are doing is different from what you ought to be doing. In the midst of messiness, *should* leads people to be stuck instead of saved, anxious instead of approaching, and guilty instead of grace-filled.

There is no perfect script to follow in a given situation. The unspoken beauty of saying just the right thing is rarely realized until long after an interaction has happened; instead, in the moment, the words simply seem like the only true thing to say. Many times, navigating a difficult situation well is less about selecting the perfect words and more about being completely present with truth and grace.

This chapter serves as a practical guide for what to do in some of the situations I hear about most often from clients, social media followers, and other people I meet along the way.

When Your Parents Have Hurt You

Parental estrangement is being increasingly discussed in my circles and the therapy space in general. For those unfamiliar with the term, it refers to adult children having problems with and becoming estranged from their parents. This is happening more often in recent years due to the widespread adoption of therapy and the weight being placed on emotions and emotional experience.

Often, parental estrangement unfolds along the following trajectory:

1. The adult child is unhappy or unwell and begins attending therapy.
2. Through the therapeutic process, the client discovers that their upbringing was not as idyllic as they thought, or they are given permission to say out loud that they were hurt, neglected, or abused as a child.
3. Having opened these wounds, the client begins to process them and reaches out to their parents for validation, acknowledgment, or repair.
4. The parents, who are woefully unprepared for this type of communication because they often haven't done their

own work, respond in a way that appears defensive, dismissive, placating, or attacking (whether intentionally or unintentionally).

5. A cycle begins in which the parent is held responsible not only for their past behavior but also for their present response to being held accountable.
6. The stakes become greater as the relationship erodes and communication falls apart.
7. Estrangement begins.

From the parents' perspective, they often report being caught off guard, unaware of the damage they have caused, and upset by the news that their child now views them as poor parents when, in their mind, they were as good as or better than any other parent of the day.

From the adult child's perspective, their parents are in denial about how things *really* were and are therefore stuck, unwilling to acknowledge the truth and move forward.

This creates an obvious stalemate in which each person believes the other party is responsible for the new problem at hand. Parents think that if their child hadn't gone to therapy, this wouldn't have happened. Adult children believe that if their parents were simply willing to accept responsibility and talk, the problem would be resolved.

Can you relate to any of this?

Chances are that you can.

Rates of parental estrangement have been growing rapidly; today, as many as 26 percent of Americans are estranged from at least one parent.[1]

It would be difficult to solve the problem of parental estrangement in just a few pages, but I'd like to try to make it easier to talk about.

For Adult Children

If you reflect on your childhood and can now see that it was more painful than you previously believed or now have confirmation that your pain is real, I see you.

It can be difficult to come to the realization that your childhood was perhaps not the one you wanted or needed. You might feel as if you've spent all your time and energy building the house of your dreams only to learn that the people who laid the foundation did so poorly and now the house must be rebuilt.

And yet, this is the cycle of life. To grow and mature means to embrace the discomfort of change; each of us experiences this to some extent because growth causes us to view things with a new perspective.

How you communicate about your growth will often determine the type of relationship you have with your parents.

Here are some guidelines for how to talk to your parents about childhood hurts:

1. Start small. Many people overlook the fact that their parents' generation often didn't discuss hard things or perhaps even feelings. So their parents are likely to get overwhelmed quickly, which may lead to a poor reaction.
2. Be clear about what hurt. Keep the list short and focus on the most impactful things.
3. Know what you want them to do in response to what you

are saying. If you don't know, keep doing your own work until you do.

4. Recognize that whatever you tell them about their failure as a parent will likely hurt them a great deal. Many (though not all) parents feel they have done the best they could. Give grace where you can.
5. Resist the urge to give an ultimatum. You can use a relationship ultimatum only once before you either must make good on it or it loses its power.
6. Recognize that your parents are unlikely to help you heal the way you'd like them to, because they don't know what you know and haven't had your experience. At best, they can respond that they love you and take responsibility, but they can't undo what's been done.

As much as your pain may be justified, it will likely take your parents longer to understand than you'd like. Communicating with grace and truth is best done when you have made significant progress toward your own healing, not when you are just learning of the problems.

The best way to ensure that your parents respond well to your feelings is to match your communication to their PATHS style and invite them into further relationship.

For Parents with Hurt Children

Part of you likely remembers what it was like to seemingly outgrow your parents—those moments when you realized you would have done things differently, your painful experiences as a child were not your fault, or the parents you had could have been better.

This is the cycle of life: raising children who are empowered and encouraged to grow, so much so that eventually they see above and beyond us. In many ways, this is an indicator of successful parenting. And yet, rather than thanking their parents for the opportunity to grow, many children today are discussing what they missed instead of what mattered.

Perhaps this cycle was easier in the past, because it played out silently. Feelings were felt and memories were processed, but nothing was spoken aloud. Perhaps remaining silent and waiting for years to express your true feelings was a better approach. Hoping but not expecting that your parents would ever understand, but moving forward anyway.

This was the approach of my parents and their parents and most likely every generation before them. Hope and wait. Say nothing but feel everything, silently.

Today things are different and children are talking. It may be different from your experience, but it's here to stay and is a healthier emotional response.

Here are guidelines for how to talk to a child who has grown up into a hurt adult:

1. Say it with me: "If it matters to them, it matters to me." Validating their emotions and acknowledging their experience is one of the most important things you can do. You don't have to agree, but you do have to acknowledge that their experience was true for them.
2. If you are unclear as to why they are upset, ask questions until you understand. And don't ask these questions through a filter of judgment, but rather from a place of curiosity.

3. Let them know when you are overwhelmed, and ask for a break or to return to the conversation later.
4. If you are willing to grow, say so. Be honest if you aren't sure what that would look like or entail. Willingness goes a long way.
5. Avoid becoming defensive or challenging your child's ideas, thoughts, or experiences. If you find yourself getting defensive, say so and take a break.
6. Instead of digging in your heels, open your arms. It is a gift to have someone care about you enough to share their pain with you—especially if the pain involves you. People only do this when they want you to make it right. This isn't an attack; it's an opportunity.

Ending a Relationship Well

Next on the list of messy situations you may need to navigate someday: What do you tell someone when a relationship is over?

Unfortunately, the "It's not you, it's me" line has been overused and is probably not going to help you out. So the first thing to realize and accept is that not every relationship lasts; many are meant for a particular season instead of being lifelong.

If you find that a relationship needs to end or has reached the close of its season, here are some guidelines:

1. Be succinct, gracious, and clear.
2. Do not use the end to complain about the beginning. If you are ending the relationship, it's already established that it wasn't working.

3. Explain your decision to the degree that it will be helpful to the person receiving the information. Recognize that most people need some kind of explanation. The best explanations start with "I feel" rather than "you." Make it clear that the explanation is not an invitation to reconsider.
4. Answer questions to the degree that it is helpful, but be aware that the longer you spend answering questions, the greater the risk that the conversation will end badly.
5. Be clear about next steps, boundaries, and further communication. Do not make the other person guess what happens next.
6. Say what you'll actually stick to, not what you "should" say.

If you are on the receiving end of someone ending a relationship with you, know that you aren't for everyone, and as painful as that may be, knowing is better than wondering. Ask what you need to ask, even if that means asking for some time to collect your thoughts.

Telling Someone That You're Hurt or Angry

How do you share with someone that they have hurt you, made you angry, or both?

First, recognize that it is okay to be hurt and angry and to tell someone.

Here are a few things to remember when sharing about your anger or hurt:

1. Don't wait until you are boiling over or can no longer stand it. Say something before you're ready to blow up.

2. Use the conflict framework we discussed earlier in the book as a guide to structure the conversation.
3. Imagine yourself entering the conversation with body armor on. The other person will likely say some things that could hurt you, but imagine that you are protected, and let some of them go.
4. Get in and get out. The goal is not to have a long discussion but instead to share how you feel and what you need.
5. Remember that not everyone deserves access to your emotions. Telling someone how you feel is a gift that not everyone will appreciate. It's important to choose wisely.

Here's the beautiful thing about telling someone that you are hurt or angry with them: It quickly demonstrates the strength and health of the relationship in real time. For instance, if the other person turns the conversation around on you or ends the relationship, you now know what an ongoing relationship would have been like. On the other hand, if you share that you have been hurt or are angry and it matters to the other person, you know you have a relationship worth building on.

Asking for Help

One of the most difficult things to do is to ask for help. I have experienced this myself and have seen it time and time again with clients. We live in a world where there is a lot of help available, but asking is the challenge.

If you are needing to ask someone for help, I see you. I know that this place can feel dark and lonely and that it often takes all the courage you have to reach out and ask.

Because of this, I want to help you reach out in a way that is most likely to result in the help you need. Here are some guidelines to walk you through the process:

1. Identify what you need help with as specifically as you can. If you aren't sure, think on it and pray about it.
2. Consider who in your circle could either help you or point you to someone who can. Sometimes the best you can do is find someone who can point you in the right direction, even if they don't have the exact experience to help you themselves.
3. Of the people who could potentially help, who are you most willing to call and ask for help today? If you need help, it's important to take action.
4. When you call, start the conversation with "I need some help with something. Do you have time to talk?" This allows the other person to understand the importance of the call and be present for you.
5. Next, tell them the general version of your story and see if they can speak into it. An example would be to tell someone that you have been struggling with addiction or depression, rather than going into all the details. If you share all the details and are met with "I'm not sure I can help," this is likely to feel like rejection or worse.
6. If the person can help, ask if you can tell them more. If they can't, ask if they're able to point you to someone who could.

You may have to ask for help more than once. In fact, it's often necessary to ask two or three times before you find someone who can help. This has nothing to do with your worth or how much people care about you. Not everyone can help you because not everyone should. Sometimes, generalists must move out of the way so you can get the specialized help you need.

If someone asks you for help, remember that this is an act of courage that few will attempt. You don't have to have all the answers; you only need to show up authentically with the person's best interest at heart.

Holding Someone Accountable

Accountability is an interesting concept, because the people who need it most often value it the least.

In brief, accountability is when we reconcile what we said we would do with what we did.

It's like the time when I told someone I'd love to help with their project, and then they called and asked me to. Or that time I told my wife I was done booking speaking engagements for the year and then approached her about adding another one.

Accountability is necessary in any relationship and is an important part of growth.

But how do you hold someone accountable?

Here are some steps to consider:

1. Start by verifying the commitment you thought the other person made.
2. If they agree that that was their commitment, ask what happened.
3. Do not argue with their reasoning. Instead, ask what prevented them from keeping their commitment.

4. Based on their answer, ask if they can still commit to what they had agreed to or if they are reconsidering their commitment.
5. Decide if their response works for you or not. Let them know either way.
6. Resist the temptation to do the other person's work, make excuses, or placate them by dropping the issue. You are worth people keeping their word.

Final Thoughts

My hope is that the information in this chapter felt both old and new at the same time. As you have learned about your PATHS type as well as other types, you have most likely developed a better understanding of how to approach conversations with greater clarity and ease.

While the conversations featured in this chapter can be very difficult, they are not too difficult for you. Approach them wisely, intentionally, and faithfully, and watch as your world begins to change.

4. Based on their answer, ask if they can still commit to what they had agreed to or if they are reconsidering their commitment.
5. Decide if their response works for you or not. Let them know either way.
6. Resist the temptation to let the other person's words make excuses or placate them by downplaying the issue. You are worthy of people keeping their word.

Final Thoughts

My hope is that the information in this chapter felt both old and new at the same time. As you have learned about your PEOPLE types as well as other types, you have most likely developed a better understanding of how to approach conversations with greater clarity and ease.

While the conversations featured in this chapter can be very difficult, they are not too difficult for you. Approach them prayerfully, intentionally, and faithfully, and watch as your world begins to change.

CHAPTER 17

Using the PATHS Framework

How to Use the PATHS Framework to Deepen Your Relationships

I hope all the things you've learned in this book are the start rather than the end of your communication journey. To get the most out of this book, consider it as both the key unlocking the door to deeper relationships, as well as the map to follow when you enter. Here's how to use it well.

1. Know Your Default Path

You will struggle profoundly to connect with others if you cannot connect to yourself. The first step to growing in your relationships is to develop insight, awareness, and understanding about yourself. Invest time in learning your dominant PATHS style and recognizing the strengths and blind spots of each path.

"Is This Court TV or Our Weekly Meeting?"

I met Randy at a business conference, and we immediately connected over our shared love of running. Randy was a leader at a busy marketing firm, and although the company was growing and he felt well-suited for his role, he told me that he often left his weekly meetings feeling like he had missed something. I asked Randy what he meant and he said, "Every week it's the same thing. I share the numbers, projections, and expectations, and as the meeting goes on people begin to look sullen and checked out." When I asked why Randy thought this was happening, he looked confused and said, "I honestly don't know. I'm giving them the facts and just being honest about my thoughts on the matter."

After Randy's last comment, I had a pretty good hunch as to what was happening. I had him take the PATHS assessment, where he scored highest on the Thinker scale. For Randy, this not only confirmed how he approached communication but also indicated why his meetings had been going so poorly. When Randy's team took the assessment, he learned that many scored lowest on the Thinker type, and the disconnect became obvious. One of Randy's employees commented that although they appreciated Randy's honesty and directness, sometimes his meetings felt more like a courtroom than a team meeting.

For Randy, knowing his default path helped him understand that others might approach the same conversation very differently. In our time working together, Randy learned how to integrate other PATHS types into his team meetings and noticed nearly immediate results. The truth didn't change, but how Randy delivered it did, and that made all the difference.

2. Recognize the Patterns in Others

Instead of reacting to your partner, teammate, friend, or family member, get curious about their communication type. Are they withdrawing because they are overwhelmed (Harbor)? Are they challenging you because they care deeply about justice (Advocate)? Are they minimizing conflict (Peacemaker)? Recognizing that others may have different PATHS styles allows you to get curious and move from taking things personally to processing things with perspective. Remember, every PATHS type makes perfect sense to the person who identifies with it, and few people set out to intentionally hurt others. Knowing this allows you to shift away from focusing only on what is said, creating an opportunity for deeper connection when you understand the other person's "why."

"When You Say It Like That, It Makes Sense"

Many couples wait a long time before seeking therapy, and Katie and Brad were no different. We met on a rainy afternoon, and both parties shared with me how disconnected they felt in their marriage. They'd started out feeling deeply connected, but now the couple could hardly speak to each other without conflict, hurt, or confusion.

"He is completely withdrawn when we are together," said Katie as she tearfully reached for a tissue. "I want connection and energy, and it just seems like Brad couldn't care less."

As Katie spoke, I noticed Brad fidgeting in his chair, and when Katie paused for Brad to respond it took a long time for him to speak. "It's not that I don't care, Katie, it's that sometimes your enthusiasm overwhelms me. I don't feel like I can keep up, so I get quiet."

Katie learned that her dominant PATHS type was Spark, and Brad's was Harbor. With this information, the dynamics of the relationship started to look different. Katie began to understand Brad's need for stability and depth, while Brad better understood Katie's need for energy and connection. As Brad looked at his assessment results, he shook his head and said that he now understood why Katie had felt so disconnected. To Brad, silence and depth were comfortable, but Katie felt very different.

Together, Brad and Katie learned to see each other through a new lens and communicate in ways that honored both of their PATHS types.

3. Learn to Translate Instead of Just Talking

Healthy communication is as much about listening as it is about talking. Each path speaks a different "language," and the more fluent you become in other styles, the better you can bridge the gap between you and the people you care about.

For example:

- Thinkers need time to process. Give them space instead of pressure.
- Sparks need engagement for connection. Respond to them with energy rather than silence.
- Peacemakers need and prioritize safety. Approach them with grace, not urgency.

When you know your type and prioritize others', connection isn't just possible; it's likely.

I met Rachel after giving a keynote address; she tearfully approached me and told me how she often felt at odds with her teenage son Cody. Rachel was gregarious and outspoken but said that whenever she spoke to Cody, she felt like he undermined her with his silence and disrespect. Rachel told me that this cycle had gone on for so long that she wondered if she and Cody would have any type of relationship after he graduated.

I encouraged Rachel to take the PATHS assessment and then schedule a call to talk about the results. When I answered the phone, Rachel could hardly wait to tell me what she had learned. "He's a Peacemaker, Jason!" she exclaimed. Rachel went on to share that she had found her primary type to be Advocate, while her son's was Peacemaker. Knowing this difference helped her see that Cody's silence wasn't about opposition but instead about overwhelm. Although Rachel's passion as an Advocate was contagious, it was also challenging to her Peacemaker son who valued agreement and harmony.

Knowing Cody's PATHS type helped Rachel soften her message, which was the catalyst to Cody opening up and the relationship growing.

4. Seek Your Own Version of Secure Communication

Each path has secure and insecure versions. When you're operating out of security, you'll find yourself able to show up for difficult conversations, practice vulnerability, and receive connection in profound ways. Security doesn't mean becoming a different person; instead, it means you can communicate in ways that are safe, grounded, and relational for you. This looks like learning to speak your truth while making room for others too.

Consider these mindset shifts:

- I have to match others' styles. → I can honor my style and accommodate theirs.
- My path makes it difficult to connect with another path. → When used with intention, my path can create connection.

Using the PATHS framework isn't about pretending to be different from who you are or abandoning your type; it's about creating safety for yourself so you can accommodate others.

Healthy relationships require the ability to both start and sustain a connection.

My friend Thomas is the type of person who lights up a room when he walks into it. Although he had a difficult upbringing, Thomas learned early on how to connect and charm to create opportunity, and his doing so has yielded several businesses and an enviable life. However, Thomas struggled frequently in romantic relationships. When he called me for advice, he admitted that his new relationship with Amber was already rocky.

"We've been having so much fun, but now she seems distant," Thomas shared as we spoke. He went on to say that he had taken Amber on several spontaneous and fun dates, but when Amber requested to stay in and talk he began to feel nervous. "I mean, what could she want to talk about? I've got tickets to the Knicks game!" For Thomas, having fun and enjoying each other's company was easy, but the prospect of sitting together and having a deep conversation seemed like a challenge, even though he was an otherwise capable person.

When Thomas learned that his primary communication type was Spark, things started to make sense. Although he was highly skilled at starting relationships and communicating for quick connection, he struggled to sustain his relationships with nurturing and deep conversations.

By working with me, Thomas learned the value of his primary type and also had the opportunity to develop his understanding of other types to have more whole and fulfilling relationships.

My dream for you is that you will use this book to create and maintain the connections you have always desired—and that along the way, you will experience changed relationships, deeper connections, and thriving in your personal and professional life more than ever before.

If nothing else, I hope you feel understood. You aren't alone, and you are far from the only one on your path.

Knowing your type means knowing there are others who see the world and communication in just the way you do. Use this information to let others know the same.

Conclusion

Together, we have reached the end of a magnificent journey. Regardless of where you started, you are further along than when you began. By now, you know your PATHS type and can most likely identify the types of those closest to you so you can speak to them in a more impactful way. And I hope you can also identify some pitfalls and obstacles that are likely to show up as you proceed on the path toward connection.

Remember, nearly everything you need to know about someone and how best to talk to them can be found in the details of your conversations if you pay attention. We are simple in the sense that our inner workings and desires are often the most common things we communicate about.

When I wrote my first book and released it into the world I felt vulnerable, insecure, and unsure. The book was well received and became the foundation for my teaching and speaking. It became part of my life to discuss my personal trauma and recall past hurts and wounds. It was normal for me to talk about experiencing abuse and struggle. But over time, my story began to lose some of the weight it once carried in my life.

One day while I was talking with a mentor, he asked me the following question:

> Of all the stories you could have written about and all the wisdom you could have shared, how did you decide to write about your past hurts?

I was struck by his question. I didn't have a great answer. I could have written a book about any subject but decided to write about my past. That was true.

After giving it some thought, I realized I told the story I did because that was the story I knew best. It's the story I had told myself in many ways over many years and during quiet moments of the night when I'd lie awake, afraid about what might happen next.

There was nothing wrong with sharing my story; in fact, it's helped lots of people and changed many lives.

But I couldn't shake the question: Why that story?

That day I realized something that Dan Allender and others have spoken about a great deal: Each of us is a reflection of the stories we tell about ourselves and the world around us.

But we can always choose a different story.

The Voice and the Vessel

At best, we are the average of the stories we tell about ourselves. And without other people to challenge or add to these stories, we often tell the same story on repeat for our whole life. It's not until we talk with others that we realize we could tell a different story.

Healthy communication is about two things:

1. **Being a Voice.** This means having a voice you are willing to share with others—being willing to communicate, speak, and advocate for what is right and true while honoring your story.
2. **Being a Vessel.** This means being humble, safe, and a conduit with whom others can talk and be honest about their stories.

The most gifted communicators can do both—and you can too.

Today could be the start of a brand-new story in which you communicate deeply and meaningfully at home and work. This story might include healthier relationships and greater awareness. It might look like you always hoped it would.

But to get the life you are called to, you must let go of the life you've had.

The first step is telling a new story.

If we learn to do this well, we can all travel together and share our stories along the way to the summit.

In 1913, Robert G. Tatum, a member of the first confirmed team to ascend Denali, reached the 20,310-foot summit and planted a makeshift flag. After grueling weeks of climbing, Tatum and his team made it, and he later described the experience as "looking out a window of heaven."[1]

I think that's a fair description of what happens when we travel together and communicate well. We get a little view of heaven here on earth.

This book could change your life if you let it—so let it.

And please let me know how it goes. Your journey matters to me.

Your friend,

Jason

Acknowledgments

When I am asked how I go about writing a book, I often find myself responding, "Incrementally, carefully, and with the support of my family." Books are not written solely by the author, but instead by the people who love them, work with them, and inspire them. This book is no different, and I am profoundly grateful to the following people for their roles in helping this book get written and launched:

To my wife, Jodi, and my children, Oliver, Isla, and Finnegan. You all know more than anyone else how much it takes to write a book, and your support has meant the world to me. You have each encouraged me, talked through ideas, and loved me well along the way, and it's made all the difference.

To Mike Vaughn, my colleague and friend. Your insights and willingness to listen and discuss this book with me are admirable. Your friendship has been life-giving, and your professional experience and feedback have strengthened me. Thank you.

To Dr. Todd Bowman, my colleague and friend. Your help working through the assessment was immensely helpful. Your ability to construct and interpret assessments that matter is a gift to many.

To Tom Dean, my literary agent at A Drop of Ink Literary. You have believed in me and advocated for me through two books, and your friendship and guidance have been instrumental in my development as an author. I am grateful for your insight and direction.

To Andrea Palpant, my editor at Zondervan. Thank you for your guidance, professionalism, and enthusiasm for this book. Your encouragement and clarity have no doubt made this project better.

To the team at Zondervan, thank you. You have advocated for me and invested in me in ways that have profoundly changed my life. I am grateful to have worked on this project together.

To my clients, who throughout the years have allowed me to walk alongside them on their journeys. It is an honor and privilege to hear the stories of your lives, relationships, and organizations. I don't take what I do lightly, and each of you has inspired me with your courage, perseverance, and desire for growth and change. I often tell people that I have the best job in the world because I get to encourage and help others while being inspired and growing in wisdom along the way. Thank you.

To my friends and family. You have all played a role in this book and taught me the power of using communication for connection. Thank you.

I also owe a great deal to the many teachers, colleagues, and mentors who have shaped the way I view people and relationships. Their insights have laid the groundwork for this book and the model within it. My hope is that my work honors the wisdom that came before me and points readers toward a deeper connection with one another and with the God who designed us for relationships.

And finally, to God. This book more than the last has felt gifted to me in the quiet times I've spent in prayer and reflection. I cannot imagine my life without my faith or the grace I receive daily. There is no better example of someone fluent in each PATHS type than Jesus, and I'm eternally inspired.

Notes

Chapter 6: Spark

1. Claudia Black, *"It Will Never Happen to Me!": Growing Up with Addiction as Youngsters, Adolescents, and Adults* (New York: Ballantine Books, 1981), 65–70.

Chapter 7: Attachment and PATHS

1. John Bowlby, *Attachment*, 2nd ed. (New York: Basic Books, 1983); Mary D. Salter Ainsworth and Sylvia M. Bell, "Attachment, Exploration, and Separation: Illustrated by the Behavior of One-Year-Olds in a Strange Situation," *Child Development* 41, no. 1 (1970): 49–67, https://doi.org/10.2307/1127388.
2. Marinus H. van IJzendoorn and Marian J. Bakermans-Kranenburg, "The Distribution of Adult Attachment Representations in Clinical and Nonclinical Groups: A Meta-Analytic Search for Patterns of Attachment in Psychopathology," *Attachment & Human Development* 8, no. 4 (2006): 371–406.

Chapter 9: Off-Ramps to Communication

1. David Rock, "SCARF: A Brain-Based Model for Collaborating with and Influencing Others," *NeuroLeadership Journal* 1 (2008): 44–52.

Chapter 10: On-Ramps to Communication

1. *APA Dictionary of Psychology*, 2nd ed. (2015), under "empathy."
2. Brené Brown, *The Gifts of Imperfection: Let Go of Who You Think You're Supposed to Be and Embrace Who You Are* (Center City, MN: Hazelden, 2010), 33.
3. Theresa Wiseman, "A Concept Analysis of Empathy," *Journal of Advanced Nursing* 23, no. 6 (1996): 1162–67, https://doi.org/10.1046/j.1365-2648.1996.12213.x.
4. Kyle Benson, "6 Hours a Week to a Better Relationship," *Gottman*, December 9, 2016, https://www.gottman.com/blog/6-hours-a-week-to-a-better-relationship.

Chapter 11: Conflict

1. Morton Deutsch, *The Resolution of Conflict: Constructive and Destructive Processes* (New Haven, CT: Yale University Press, 1973), 10.
2. "Most Skips of a Skimming Stone," Guinness World Records, September 6, 2013, https://www.guinnessworldrecords.com/world-records/most-skips-of-a-skimming-stone.
3. Michael Fulwiler, "Managing Conflict: Solvable vs. Perpetual Problems," *Gottman*, updated July 2, 2025, https://www.gottman.com/blog/managing-conflict-solvable-vs-perpetual-problems.

Chapter 12: Saying Hard Things

1. Henry Cloud and John Townsend, *Boundaries: When to Say Yes, How to Say No to Take Control of Your Life*, updated ed. (Grand Rapids, MI: Zondervan, 2017).
2. Terri Cole, *Boundary Boss: The Essential Guide to Talk True, Be Seen, and (Finally) Live Free* (Oakland, CA: Sounds True, 2020).

Chapter 13: Practicing Communication

1. Laurnie Wilson, "Asking for Help May Be a Privilege," *CivicScience*, September 13, 2018, https://civicscience.com/asking-for-help-may-be-a-privilege/.

2. "'Stigma Effect' Stops Three in Five People Experiencing Mental Illness from Seeking Help, Survey Reveals," Rethink Mental Illness, May 15, 2023, https://www.rethink.org/news-and-stories/media-centre/2023/05/stigma-effect-stops-three-in-five-people-experiencing-mental-illness-from-seeking-help-survey-reveals/.
3. Natalie Doan, Karen A. Patte, Mark A. Ferro, and Scott T. Leatherdale, "Reluctancy Towards Help-Seeking for Mental Health Concerns at Secondary School Among Students in the COMPASS Study," *International Journal of Environmental Research and Public Health* 17, no. 19 (September 29, 2020): 7128, https://pubmed.ncbi.nlm.nih.gov/33003499/.
4. Alan Richardson, "Mental Practice: A Review and Discussion, Part I," *Research Quarterly for Exercise and Sport* 38, no. 1 (1967): 95–107.

Chapter 14: Responding to Hard Things

1. Albert Mehrabian and Susan R. Ferris, "Inference of Attitudes from Nonverbal Communication in Two Channels," *Journal of Consulting Psychology* 31, no. 3 (1967): 248–52, https://psycnet.apa.org/doi/10.1037/h0024648. The frequently cited 93 percent figure—55 percent body language, 38 percent tone of voice, 7 percent words—comes from combining this and other Mehrabian studies, and applies specifically to communication about feelings and attitudes, not to all communication contexts.

Chapter 16: Special Circumstances

1. Avrum Weiss, "Unpacking the Epidemic of Parental Estrangement," *Psychology Today*, May 19, 2024, https://www.psychologytoday.com/us/blog/from-fear-to-intimacy/202405/unpacking-the-epidemic-of-parental-estrangement.

Conclusion

1. Patrick Dean, *A Window to Heaven: The Daring First Ascent of Denali: America's Wildest Peak* (New York: Pegasus Books, 2021).

From the Publisher

GREAT BOOKS

ARE EVEN BETTER WHEN THEY'RE SHARED!

Help other readers find this one

- Post a review at your favorite online bookseller
- Post a picture on a social media account and share why you enjoyed it
- Send a note to a friend who would also love it—or better yet, give them a copy

Thanks for reading!